THE ESSENCE OF CHRISTIANITY

THE ESSENCE OF CHRISTIANITY

A fresh look at the Nicene Creed

Brian Hebblethwaite

First published in Great Britain 1996
Society for Promoting Christian Knowledge
Holy Trinity Church
Marylebone Road
London NW1 4DU

Biblical quotations are from *The Revised English Bible* (REB) © 1989
Oxford and Cambridge University Presses.

British Library Cataloguing-in-Publication Data

A catalogue record of this book is available from
the British Library

ISBN 0-281-04815-0

Typeset by Pioneer Associates, Perthshire
Printed in Great Britain by
Biddles Ltd., Guildford and Kings Lynn

For Emma and Alexandra

Contents

The Nicene Creed

We believe in one God,
the Father, the Almighty,
maker of heaven and earth,
of all that is, seen and unseen.

We believe in one Lord, Jesus Christ,
the only Son of God,
eternally begotten of the Father,
God from God, Light from Light,
true God from true God,
begotten, not made,
of one Being with the Father;
through him all things were made.
For us and for our salvation
he came down from heaven,
was incarnate of the Holy Spirit and the Virgin Mary
and became a human being.
For our sake he was crucified under Pontius Pilate;
he suffered death and was buried.
On the third day he rose again
in accordance with the Scriptures;
he ascended into heaven
and is seated at the right hand of the Father.
He will come again in glory to judge the living and the dead,
and his kingdom will have no end.
We believe in the Holy Spirit, the Lord, the giver of life,
who proceeds from the Father [and the Son],
who with the Father and the Son is worshipped and glorified,

who has spoken through the prophets.
We believe in one holy catholic and apostolic Church.
We acknowledge one baptism for the forgiveness of sins.
We look for the resurrection of the dead,
and the life of the world to come. Amen.

Introduction

Nearly forty years ago, John Burnaby gave two series of lectures in Cambridge on the Nicene Creed, which were later published as *The Belief of Christendom* (SPCK 1959), a book which remained in print for many years. It proved extremely helpful to students and to the general reader, enabling them to see the wood for the trees and to get a clear, yet penetrating, overview of the central beliefs of the Christian Churches. Behind it lay a lifetime of study and teaching; yet the learning remained in the background, and the reader was given an immediately intelligible and coherent, as well as authoritative, presentation of the essence of Christianity, as formulated and handed down in the Christian creeds.

This is a task required of every generation and I welcome the opportunity to have another go at setting out the meaning of the Creed and defending its claim to truth. Mine will be a much less close commentary on the Nicene Creed than Burnaby's, though I am glad that it is the Nicene Creed that still provides the focus for my own exposition. For this is the Creed which Christians say in the course of the Eucharist, the main act of Christian worship. Much has been written of the place of creeds in worship, but, while recognizing that context and its importance for reflection on the content of the Creed, I shall not myself be emphasizing the Creed as worship. Like Burnaby, I am interested in the truth content of Christian belief and its credibility in today's world.

This means that a great deal of attention has to be given to contemporary culture and the climate of opinion that

3

characterizes our modern world, especially our modern western world. It is a commonplace that we live in a secular age. And just as an earlier 'age of faith' made the Christianity of the creeds more plausible to the population at large, so an age of unbelief like ours makes atheism or at least agnosticism the more plausible option. These broadly sociological factors operate both ways. But we are not interested in plausibility. We are interested in truth. And even in a climate of unbelief, the Christianity of the creeds may still in fact contain the truth about the world, about ourselves and about the future. It may need much more digging out and explaining than it used to do, but there is still the possibility that one can find embedded here in the Christian tradition the clue to the meaning of life.

Nevertheless, in investigating this possibility, we shall have to pay a great deal of attention to why it is that so many of our contemporaries find Christian belief, and especially belief in a God of love, difficult, if not impossible. In this connection we shall want to ponder the factors that have led so many to reject the old certainties and the old authorities, and to think of themselves as self-sufficient, whether just as products of society or as free, autonomous beings, able to create their own lives and their own worlds.

We shall, of course, be reflecting on the threat which modern science allegedly poses to religion and especially to the idea that God is active in the world. We shall also have to keep in mind the vast problem of evil and suffering in a world allegedly created by a good, all-powerful God. This is the most often-cited difficulty – by ordinary folk and by professors of philosophy alike – with Christian belief in God.

Then the very intelligibility of the notion of God is questioned by many people today. What sense can be given to the idea of infinite, incorporeal, yet personal Spirit, both transcendent to and immanent in, the whole cosmos? This is perhaps a more esoteric difficulty. For the man or woman in the street, whether believer or unbeliever, tends to have in mind a rather more anthropomorphic picture of God, perhaps derived from a literal reading of the Bible.

Mention of the Bible raises the whole question of our modern recognition of the cultural and historical strangeness of those texts coming down to us from thousands of years ago. Can they still function as holy Scripture, and what might that mean in a critical age like ours? The creeds have never been invested with quite such an aura of sanctity as the Bible has, but similar problems arise concerning the creeds' authority and relevance. Their language and their thought-forms are not ours. Historical criticism has shown how much they too are products of ancient, seemingly superseded, civilizations, and of controversies long since buried.

There are other, more specific, problems of intelligibility that people have about the Christianity of the creeds. The doctrines of the Trinity and incarnation are found extremely hard to understand not only by unbelievers but by religious people more familiar with the great monotheistic faiths of Judaism and Islam. And even many Christians themselves are inclined to admit to finding these doctrines pretty obscure. Unitarian, non-incarnational, versions of Christianity are increasingly popular today.

Mention of Judaism and Islam opens up the whole problem of other religions. This too is part of the contemporary context in which we come to examine the historic creeds of Christianity. For we are much more aware of the great riches of spirituality and faith fostered not only in the other religions of semitic origin but also in the religions of the east, the far east, and of Africa. No commentary on the Nicene Creed today can ignore the fascinating history of religions, world-wide – other scriptures, other prophets and gurus, other ways of life and worship, other, conflicting, truth claims. We cannot avoid the question of how much these different faiths have in common, and of how far the Christian faith, summed up in the Nicene Creed, represents a distinctive and unique revelation, opening up a vision of God and his purpose for the future of creation that goes beyond all other revelations and visions of ultimate reality and ultimate meaning.

But there are also more pragmatic sorts of difficulty to be faced. The long history of Christianity and the actual practice of Christians, past and present, are so ambiguous. Many people are more conscious of the horrors perpetrated in the name of Christianity – the Crusades, the Inquisition, the

wars of religion, ethnic and communal conflicts bolstered by
different forms of Christianity, and, not least, the ethical out-
rageousness of some of the beliefs themselves that Christians
have held or still hold – belief in everlasting damnation in
the fires of hell, to cite but one example – than they are of
the undoubted benefits brought to humanity by the Christian
religion. I shall have much to say later on about those benefits – the many different forms of creativity, life-enhancement
and love of the neighbour that we owe to Christianity. But the
negative side of the picture is pretty bleak. The world does
not look redeemed. And where Christianity itself is seen to
have fostered hatred, insensitivity and the lie instead of love,
vision and truth, no wonder people turn against it and look
for some allegedly more humanistic alternative.

These negative effects of what, of course, I shall be claiming is the abuse of Christianity are one reason why I shall be
stressing at every stage the positive ethical implications and
indeed effects of the doctrines of the Creed, when they are
properly understood and appropriated, both inwardly and
outwardly. But again I have to stress that my main concern in
this book is the question of the truth of Christian doctrine. I
hope to show, too, that it is the actual content of Christian
belief as expressed in the Nicene Creed that necessarily implies
and gives rise to very distinctive ethical ideals regarding the
personal and interpersonal lives of individuals as well as the
forms of human community, and at the same time sums up
the spiritual resources that are actually available to people
and society for the realization of these ideals.

The understanding of credal Christianity offered here is
just one person's attempt to show that, notwithstanding the
hostile or indifferent secular mentality of the modern west,
notwithstanding the power and success of modern science,
notwithstanding the terrible problem of evil and suffering
in the world, notwithstanding the difficulties of historical and
philosophical credibility posed by our modern critical self-
consciousness, notwithstanding our contemporary awareness
of other profound religions and philosophies of life, and notwithstanding our ethical revulsion at what religion, including
Christianity, has often been responsible for, notwithstanding
all this, the Christian faith that came to expression in the

Nicene Creed still represents perhaps the most compelling as well as the most wide-ranging vision of the world and human life, and of their meaning and their destiny.

My account of this positive vision is bound to be partial and idiosyncratic at certain points. There are many other ways in which the essence of Christianity can be understood and explained. After all, Christianity is a very large and all-embracing affair. Inevitably, over time, it has divided into varying strands, not just the different Churches and denominations, with their differing slants on the heart of the matter, but each strand embracing differing perceptions of what it is all about. I hope that my exposition is a reasonably balanced and central one and that at the same time I can succeed in showing what most Christians have in common, but I cannot possibly claim that credal Christianity can only be understood this way. I shall try to indicate, from time to time, the range of possible interpretations of the more controversial elements in the Nicene Creed that Christians might reasonably adopt or be permitted to adopt by the Churches which exist to hand the faith on from generation to generation. Occasionally I shall mention some interpretations canvassed today that are really beyond the pale and constitute so radical a break with historical Christianity as not to count as possible or permissible versions of Christian faith in any meaningful sense. One of the reasons why we retain the historic creeds – and of course the holy Scriptures – is to maintain continuity down the ages. And continuity matters just because we believe that this *historic* faith encapsulates the truth.

The claim that historic Christianity encapsulates the truth – and that means the ultimate truth about God, the universe and human nature and destiny – is entirely bound up with the conviction that the God of all the earth has revealed to humankind, in human history, the divine reality, the divine nature and the divine purpose underlying our world and shaping its final goal. The creeds sum up Christian understanding of that revelation. But although I shall be concerned, throughout this book, with the heart of this alleged revelation, I shall not be presenting it simply in a take it or leave it manner. At every stage, I shall not only be arguing with unbelief, but trying to indicate the points in common between Christianity and religion and philosophy world-wide. And even where Christianity, as in its doctrines of the Trinity and incarnation, is unique, affirming a revelation that transcends all others, this too will be argued for, and spelled out in terms that attempt to show the sense it makes and the vision of reality it opens up. The truth of Christianity must be allowed to commend itself to the head as well as to the heart, and show itself as a compelling world view as well as an inspiring way of life, and the chief source of hope for the world.

CHAPTER ONE

Today's World

A PLURALISTIC WORLD

We have come, in the late twentieth century, to think and speak of our world as one world – space-ship Earth, the global village, a communicational unity in which events, politics and cultures, statesmen, musicians and sports personalities from all over the world are presented day after day on our television screens and in the press as elements in a single story. Never before has so much information about Earth and its inhabitants been so universally available. And never before have an interest and a sense of participation in what is going on in every corner of the globe been forced upon us so insistently. Moreover we have become aware of the closely interwoven ecological structure of life on Earth and the conditions that make it possible. Not only the human story, but the whole story of life, has acquired an all-embracing unity.

Yet the more we become aware of this fragile and precarious planet as a single home for all species of life, the more we recognize the extraordinary variety of the populations, cultures, political systems and individuals that make up the most complex and highly developed of those species, *homo sapiens*. Our human world is truly a pluralistic world. Despite the pervasive influence, world-wide, of modern science and technology, the civilizations of Europe, of India and South-East Asia, of China, and of the Arab world, to name but a few, retain and indeed re-emphasize their different and distinct ways of being human. Moreover, each major section of humanity is found to contain a truly astonishing variety, not only in terms of ethnicity and nationhood, but also of sub-cultures and life-styles within any single country or region.

This fascinating variety has a grim side to it, as we are all only too well aware. Tribalism in post-colonial Africa, communalism in India, the revival of nationalisms in eastern Europe and the former Soviet Union, ethnic cleansing in the Balkans, have shown how dangerous and destructive this potent sense of group identity can be, where relations with other communities and groups are in question. Internally, of course, these factors play a very positive part in creating and fostering the cultures and identities that colour the human scene in such amazingly diverse ways.

Many such communities remain, internally, relatively uniform in terms of attitudes and ways of life, but in the larger countries of Europe, North America and Australasia, we find a prodigious internal pluralism. The United States is, notoriously, the most striking example of a country which, largely because it lacks a long history and is made up of numerous immigrant populations, embraces a great diversity of ethnic groups, subcultures and styles of life. One of its most positive features is the relative success with which it has made a virtue out of pluralism and managed, despite a terrible civil war in the nineteenth century, to forge a single nation out of such diverse material. Tolerance of diversity has not come easily even there. Dominant majorities – or even minorities – have, from time to time, endeavoured to impose a single 'American dream'; but at least the United States has kept together, and, sustained by its great energy and dynamism, shown the possibility of diversity in unity on a pretty large scale.

Later in this chapter we shall be considering the place of *religious* pluralism on the world scene. Religion has often been a unifying force, providing a single 'umbrella of meaning' for particular communities, nations, or even civilizations. Many religions have attempted to tell, each from its own standpoint, a single story about the world and humankind, from the beginning; but none of them, not even the great 'world' religions, has succeeded in doing this on a truly global scale. Now that we have indeed achieved a global perspective through modern communications, we are more aware of religious diversity, and of the difficulty – some would say impossibility – of seeing, from within a particular religious horizon, universal history as a single meaningful process. And indeed, as mentioned in the introduction, many of our contemporaries are more conscious of religion as a divisive force, reinforcing ethnic or sectarian intolerance, sometimes to the most horrific and violent extremes.

One of the tasks of this book will be to try to see whether the Christianity of the creeds, despite all this plurality, still has the power to foster and sustain a unified vision of the world and of world history, including the history of religions.

A SECULAR AGE

But, first, we must consider the view that religion is on the way out. The so-called 'secularization thesis' holds that, especially in the west, but increasingly world-wide, religion is being marginalized by the rise of modern science and its technological applications on a vast scale to the structures of human life. In any case, more and more social institutions – education, health care, even charities – are now run on secular lines; and we have become used to the idea of 'morality without religion'. But it is science and its products that have most changed attitudes to the world about us and to the way things work. Our everyday lives, more often than not, involve no reference to religion. When the car breaks down, few resort seriously to prayer.

It is easy to exaggerate the secularization thesis, however. For one thing the media are probably more secularized than the majority of the population, even in a country like Britain, where attendance in churches is pretty low. Journalists and television reporters tend to treat religious phenomena as quaint survivals and genuinely religious people as bizarre freaks. But media men and women are hardly representative and they are as clearly conditioned by their particular environment as anyone else. In fact there is a great deal of religion, ranging from the bizarre to the very profound, even in the most secularized western nations. Christianity may have ceased to provide a common framework of meaning for all citizens in a country like Britain, but serious Christian commitment is not hard to find among politicians, students, working scientists, and people on the street. Practising Christians may be a minority, but then serious Christian faith and practice have probably always been a minority business, even in the so-called 'ages of faith', when Christianity did provide the framework of ideas within which social life was lived.

Where measurable religious phenomena are concerned – such as church attendance and membership of religious organizations – the statistics vary enormously between, for example, England and Ireland, France, Sweden, the United States, and Poland; and it is interesting to speculate about the factors, often political and geopolitical, that lie behind these differences. The role of the Churches in the break-up of communism in eastern Europe is a fascinating case-study here. But one factor is relatively new: the presence of sometimes large minorities from other traditions of faith, Muslim, Hindu, Sikh and, of course, Jewish – a pretty ancient presence in western Europe and, in so far as anything is ancient there, in the United States as well. And with the breakdown of the common 'public' framework provided by Christianity in the past, there has undoubtedly been a kind of privatization of religion into a variety of faith communities, including the various Christian Churches. The process has been taken further by smaller groups and individuals, attracted either by other religions, especially Buddhism, or by new religions (a particularly Japanese phenomenon), or by the curiously rootless New Age movements, which attempt to invent religion afresh for a scientific age.

All this goes to show that a considerable quantity of religion (and religion substitutes, of which I have said nothing yet) flourishes even in the secular west. And although the influence of western science and technology is world-wide and irreversible, large sections of the rest of the world have shown a much greater resistance to the erosion of the hold of religion on the public domain than has been the case in the west. This is especially true of the Muslim world, where the power of Islamic fundamentalism is increasingly seen as a factor to be reckoned with. But it is also true of Hindu revivalism in India, and, to a degree, of Buddhism in South-East

Asia, Sri Lanka and Tibet (although, perforce, it is the exiles who make the running there).

If the secularization thesis looks so shaky, from a western as well as from a global perspective, notwithstanding the collapse of the single common framework that one associates with the term 'Christendom' (one could not give a book like this the title *The Belief of Christendom* today), and if religion, in one form or another, looks like being here to stay, we shall need to ask ourselves what factors prompt the widespread dissatisfaction with modern secularity. What is it that induces disillusion with the omnicompetence of science? What drives people back to the old faiths or inclines them to experiment with the new? In the sections that follow, we shall explore some of the inadequacies of a purely scientific view of the world, but also of a purely humanistic one. Eventually we shall be asking whether the old faiths, and in particular the Christianity of the creeds, are not better placed to meet these felt or discerned inadequacies so prevalent today.

SCIENCE AND TECHNOLOGY

That the world has been transformed by the applications of modern scientific knowledge needs no arguing. I have already mentioned how general attitudes to the way things work are largely determined by this ever-increasing knowledge and its popularization through education and the media, but, above all, through the universal use of the technologies and their products that modern science has made possible. But scientific theory, too, continues to fascinate. Developments in evolutionary theory as well as in molecular biology hold out the prospect of showing in more and more detail how humankind has emerged from the animal world and how specifically human characteristics are passed on from generation to generation. Developments in computer science hold out the prospect of simulating and thus explaining the human mind and human intelligence. Developments in cosmology and elementary particle physics hold out the prospect of our coming up with a unified theory of everything, which will explain the basic capacities of physical energy to produce, through cosmic evolution, the life-supporting systems that we know – and to do so, it seems, without requiring a beginning or a boundary, to the whole physical universe.

Science and technology are largely western products and account for the influence, even dominance, of the west worldwide. They account too, in large measure, for the secularity of our modern age. But, as already intimated, their omnicompetence is increasingly challenged. Practically speaking, science and technology appear to have overreached themselves. Far from solving the problems of organizing, sustaining and enriching the Earth's human population, they are now seen to be exacerbating overpopulation, depleting non-renewable resources, upsetting the ecological balance of nature, equipping the bellicose with ever more destructive weaponry, culminating in the nuclear threat that may put an end to the whole human story. Theoretically speaking, the quest for universal explanations in terms of the fundamental laws of physics is increasingly felt to be not so much threatening as wholly implausible. It is not surprising that students tend to opt for arts courses and to look down on science as something of mere utilitarian value – and that only in the short term – compared with the riches of history and literature and the creative arts. Even the exciting developments on the frontiers of theoretical science that I mentioned just now show little sign of being able to explain such fundamental facts of experience as consciousness, thought, freedom and reason, to say nothing of creativity, personality and love. The forms of interpersonal relation, of communal life and culture, whose plurality I began by emphasizing in the opening section of this chapter, are simply not captured, still less explained, by the natural, or even the social sciences.

Among the factors central to human life in the past, and still to a considerable extent today, that escape and transcend the nets of scientific explanation is religion – the whole world of spirituality, mysticism, prayer and worship. But the historical religions, including Christianity, come down to us from the pre-scientific ages, and they have, of course, had to adjust and come to terms with the scientific revolution. I shall be arguing, especially in chapter four on creation, that the Christian faith is well placed to take modern cosmology and evolutionary theory in its stride. Not surprisingly, the mythical form of pre-scientific cosmologies and anthropologies that we find in the Scriptures and to a much lesser extent in the creeds, has to be discarded or shown to express, in pre-scientific picture-language, underlying doctrines and beliefs quite capable of expression in terms that take account of modern science. The core doctrines of the Christian creeds speak of ultimate origins, divine revelation, true human nature, the meaning of life and of the whole world process, the spiritual resources for transforming what is wrong with humanity, and the final destiny of creation and of us all – questions that the sciences cannot even begin to answer. Whatever success they have in unlocking the secrets of nature's composition, basic laws and causal interactions, they do not begin to account for the very existence of a complex energy field, and its capacity to evolve such remarkable phenomena as life, mind, interpersonal relation and culture.

Once we see that scientific explanation can only operate within certain given parameters, we can go on to appreciate the need to keep science and technology under ethical control. The whole domain of morality is a key instance of the values and value systems that go beyond the scope of science. And only if the prior claims of morality are recognized can the destructive effects of science and technology, mentioned just now, be curtailed or prevented. This is clear in the case of medical ethics, where some ethical control over the application of advances, say, in genetics, is undeniably required.

Both theoretically and practically, therefore, we are led to recognize the limitations of science and technology and to acknowledge the domains of religion and ethics, of ultimate explanation and moral obligation.

AUTONOMY

Even more basic to the spirit of today's world than the influence of science and technology is the Enlightenment's insistence on human autonomy, on our ability and duty to think and legislate for ourselves, rather than rely on the traditional authorities. The growth of modern science was itself an example of this. But even where the limitations of science are recognized, creativity and the affirmation of value are still widely regarded as free human projects and activities. In this sense the human race is held to have come of age, and accepted its true nature as a self-legislator and creator of the human world and all its different values. Much existentialist philosophy exemplifies this strong sense of autonomy.

Some aspects of this stress on human autonomy are indeed quite justified. People should think for themselves, accept responsibility for their acts and policies, and internalize and make their own the values of morality, art and culture. We do not want, nor ought we, to follow the herd, to accept only second-hand opinions, or to live by convention alone. But the idea that human beings create value, and that it is up to them to fashion an ideal of life by which to live, has led to very damaging consequences in the modern world. It has led to a pervasive moral relativism and undermined the common moral vocabulary that used to reinforce people's sense of right and wrong. Instead of argument and sober reflection, we get diverse expressions of opinion and the formation of rival pressure groups. The idea that moral truth is something to be discovered, learned and inwardly appropriated is abandoned in favour of what is claimed as the affirmation of 'my' truth or 'your' truth. Whether this takes an extreme individualist form or a more social form, with different subgroups within the wider society mutually reinforcing their members' collective attitudes, the result is the same: not only the loss of a common morality, but a diminution of conscience, and of the recognition of obligations under which all human beings stand simply in virtue of being human. It is ironic that, in an age where many people demonstrate a strong commitment to human rights world-wide, the objective basis for such commitment is being widely abandoned. It thus becomes all the easier for individuals and groups to let other commitments and other ideologies override human rights. This has even happened in the case of some extreme advocates of animal 'rights'.

Human freedom is indeed a great value, integral to being a person, with all the rights and responsibilities that that entails. It is integral to thought, action, interpersonal relation, and all the communal and cultural forms of life that make human existence the fascinating and inherently valuable thing that it is. Later in this book we shall be considering this freedom in the context of God's creation. It is part of the image of God in humanity, part of what distinguishes the human from the other animals. The importance of the gift of freedom will be stressed when we try to understand why evil is permitted in God's world. But the freedom and autonomy that characterize our human nature are not absolute. Indeed when thought of and treated as absolute, human autonomy arrogates to itself the prerogatives of God and becomes the source of much illusion and evil, as the myth of Prometheus shows.

Our true freedom and autonomy are to be found precisely in relation to a given environment, including the other people with whom we find ourselves in relation, and, it will be argued, in relation to the God who made us. People's rights and responsibilities in relation to each other are central aspects of the situations in which they *find* themselves, situations which make claims on a person quite objectively and categorically. And the fact that human autonomy, when absolutized, leads to relativism, amoralism and even contradiction, is yet another pointer to the need for a theology that makes sense of moral obligation and objective value.

NIHILISM

These last remarks may seem rather extravagant. Surely, it may be replied, the ethical relativism and subjectivism that have come to prevail in the wake of the Enlightenment's stress on human autonomy are not so devastating in their consequences as I have just made out. Apologists for secular liberal pluralism argue that on fundamental matters like observing the basic necessary conditions of life together in society and caring for children, the elderly and the sick, most people think and behave ethically, without any reference to or support from religion. It is not too difficult, they say, to socialize new generations into recognizing and observing these basic norms of human behaviour since they correspond so obviously to human nature and needs. Over and above this shared framework for life together, variety in ideals and styles of life is a good thing, enriching the human scene. By contrast, the extremities of nihilism, the belief that, where God is dead, anything is possible and nothing matters, is a bizarre unnatural product of the more extreme forms of continental philosophy.

One might wish that this relatively cheerful liberal view were true, but the fact is that the loss of a more pervasive, all-embracing, common framework of shared values and obligations, and of their grounding in the nature and will of God, has led to a much more serious breakdown, even collapse, of the sense of right and wrong among large sections of the population. It has not proved as easy as optimistic educators thought to socialize new generations, least of all the under-privileged *and* the privileged, into respecting and observing even the basic necessary conditions of social life. And once a society's system of values is felt to have no deeper basis than that of being the best framework for the maximization of preferences, and once the sanctions of morality are felt to be no more than those of common prudence – one obviously tries to avoid being caught – it is only too easy for individuals to pursue their own ends ruthlessly without regard for other people.

This nihilistic trend is manifested not only in increased crime, drug abuse, vandalism and aggressive behaviour generally, nor just in the apparent lack of guilt or conscience in those apprehended, but also in the casual attitudes to abortion, sexual relations, family commitments and the care of the mentally sick that characterize much, at least, of modern western society. There are not only far too many exceptions to the liberal view that people in general share a sense of fairness and an overall benevolence; but also the liberal consensus itself inclines towards managerial rather than ethical attitudes to such problems as the deployment of resources in health care and how to deal with misfits, the marginalized and the utterly helpless.

So, we are faced, particularly in the west, with a pretty shaky liberal system of values, that lacks the wherewithal to commend itself through education and socialization to new generations, even regarding the basic conditions of life together in community. And where ideals of life and private value systems are concerned, there is no common language and no rational means of settling moral disputes. In this climate of assertion and counter-assertion, tempered only by managerial techniques and social engineering, ruthless egoism drives many individuals and gangs to ride roughshod over other people, often with appalling violence, not only in order to achieve their own ends, but, also, it seems, for pleasure.

It is in this context of a weakened overall value system in public life, of irreconcilable preferences and life-styles in private life, and of strong nihilistic tendencies at many points, both public and private, that we are perhaps driven back to religion as a possible source of meaning and value for all aspects of our life together.

A SENSE OF HISTORY

One of the least attractive features of the modern age is its repudiation of history and tradition. It is not that we lack an interest in history. The past fascinates us. But just as dinosaurs have little or no connection with our own twentieth-century styles of life, so past ages of human history, like distant cultures today, seem only to be of aesthetic interest. Even the nineteenth century in one's own country appears like foreign territory as far as attitudes to the world and values by which to live are concerned. So much is new and different that people feel that they have nothing to learn from the past. Even where it is held that human self-confidence, born of the Enlightenment and the success of science and technology, has broken down, the subcultures and counter-cultures that attract are, for the most part, new. And even where they are gleaned from elements in the ancient world religions, it is usually the non-historical, cosmic philosophies of the east and the far east that are assumed to hold the key to a peaceful and harmonious existence.

The great exception to this rejection of history as a source of meaning in life is nationalism. For many peoples, especially in situations of relative oppression, it is their national or ethnic identity, sustained by a particular language and culture and by a long history, often of suffering, that gives them a powerful sense of meaning and purpose, and enables them, at an opportune moment, such as the collapse of communism, to claim statehood or even to form new states. In many parts of the world, however, political autonomy is not a possibility nor necessarily the best thing for the peoples concerned. We have already noted the disasters that have followed upon the assertion of such unrestrained nationalisms in the Balkans and elsewhere. And such has been the terrible history of international conflict in the past that the states of western Europe, whose geography and history have for a time favoured the pursuit of national identities, have now turned in a different direction to a new kind of internationalism. Of course it is all too easy for peoples with a long history of national self-assertion to forsake such mutually destructive ideologies and to look askance at the aspirations of others. But there is no denying the demonic character of nationalism absolutized.

Religion has often reinforced nationalism, investing it with just those absolute, unqualified, claims that have caused, and still cause, havoc in the relations of different peoples with one another. But a religion can only count as a world religion if, whatever its origins, it transcends nationalism and enables and sustains, *sub specie aeternitatis*, a critical perspective on all purely human achievements, including all social and communal forms of life. Ideally, Christianity, not least in its Roman Catholic forms and through the World Council of Churches, should be a moderating influence where nationalist passions are concerned.

The Christianity of the creeds may hope to temper and relativize particular national and ethnic identities, and to transcend purely local histories; but it can have no truck with the repudiation of history and tradition which, nationalism apart, is characteristic of modern, science-based, cultures, especially in the west. Christianity is itself a historical religion, not only in the sense that it comes down to us over two millennia, but in the sense that it encourages us to think of universal history as a meaningful process, with the final clue to the meaning of history and of human life having been given at a particular time in the past. As we shall see, the fact that its claimed unique and final revelation took place two thousand years ago in an obscure corner of the Roman Empire is no barrier to its contemporary relevance and appropriation in the modern age. On the contrary, just because modernity has so conspicuously failed us on the scores of meaning and morality, we need to look again at the wisdom of the past and the traditions that convey that wisdom to us down the generations. Certainly the historic faith has to be related to the undeniable discoveries of modern science. It has to pass through the fires of critical scrutiny. But we shall be exploring the Christianity of the creeds in this book precisely in order to see whether, duly purged and reformulated in the light of scientific discoveries and historical criticism, it still has the spiritual and rational resources not only to explain but also to illuminate and transform human life on earth.

THE PHENOMENON OF RELIGION

Despite all the factors that make us speak of this as a secular age, religion shows little sign of withering away. And despite all that can be said about the dangerous ideological reinforcement which it sometimes gives to rampant nationalism, the main significance of religion on the human scene is readily perceived to lie elsewhere. In their various ways the religions, at their best, have met certain deep psychological needs for integration and meaning in personal life. They have fulfilled certain pervasive sociological functions, promoting group solidarity and investing corporate life with an overarching meaning. They have inspired and sustained deeply ethical ways of life at both the personal and the communal level. And they have offered overall interpretations of the world and of human life as sustained by and orientated towards a transcendent and eternal source, background or goal.

Some have taken a cosmic, even cyclical, form, evoking a spirituality of oneness with nature, with all sentient life, or with ultimate reality conceived in impersonal, all-pervasive, absolute terms. Others have taken a more linear, historical form, suggesting that we are all part of a developing process, leading towards a perfected consummation in the end, a consummation willed by a personal God, the source and

goal of everything. Both types, at least where the great world
religions are concerned, include profound analyses of what is
wrong with the human condition and what spiritual resources
are available to men and women to gain them liberation or
salvation. This transformation is of course variously conceived, sometimes in more individual, sometimes in more
social, ways. But there is no doubt that the religions, over the
centuries, despite the abuses which loom so large in secular
consciousness, have provided countless millions with conso-
lation, a sense of meaning and purpose, a hope for the future,
and the spiritual resources to bring good out of evil and new
life out of despair. Not infrequently, too, they have produced
saintly lives and communities of quite extraordinary depth
and power.

All this still goes on today, but in an increasingly unfriendly
environment. And of course the sixty-four-thousand dollar
question remains, even when we concentrate on the positive,
beneficial, contributions of religion to the good of humankind, whether these ancient faiths are merely products or
projections of the human mind – collective instances of
wish fulfilment, perhaps – or whether, indeed, they represent
human responses to the transcendent and genuine windows
into eternity.

The phenomenon of religion in the history of the world
and the fact of religious experience of so many different, yet
comparable kinds – awe, mysticism, illumination, universal
gratitude, a sense of sin and forgiveness, inspiration and
hope against hope – pose fundamental questions of truth. It
is not just a question of whether these things can be given a
psychological or sociological explanation. The strength or
weakness of secular or purely humanist interpretations of
religion is linked to the strength or weakness of secularism,
whether science-based or humanist, in general. If there are
good reasons for supposing that the very existence of the
physical universe can only be explained in terms of some
absolute necessary ground, and if the capacity of the basic
energy-field, under the precise, mathematically expressible,
laws of nature to produce, through cosmic and biological
evolution, worlds of life, including rational, personal, beings
like ourselves, can only be explained in terms of intelligence

and purpose behind the whole story, then the history of religious experience has some claim to be taken seriously as the history of our encounter with that transcendent source of all finite being and value.

It will not be possible to include much comparative study of religion in this book, but as we explore the main themes of the Christian creed, we shall need to bear these wider questions in mind – how much common ground there is between the great world faiths, how distinctive credal Christianity is, and how successful Christian theology of religion can be in making sense, from its own perspective, of the phenomenon of religion world-wide.

RELIGION SUBSTITUTES

I shall say little about the new religions, cults and New Age movements which represent so marked a reaction against the Enlightenment project and the omnicompetence of scientific materialism. Interesting as they are to the sociologist of religion, and testimony though they bear to the power of the religious impulse and the need for religion in human life, they are far too narrow, exclusive and irrational to be taken seriously. It is impossible to find in them profound world views capable of making sense of all aspects of human history and experience. They cannot plausibly be related to modern scientific knowledge, nor can they embrace the kind of critical self-scrutiny and reformulation that the great world religions – to differing degrees – have proved themselves capable of doing. They lack explanatory force, ethical and spiritual profundity and the power to foster an open and creative human community, and they lack a realistic hope for the future of creation.

Much the same has to be said about the religion substitutes that, for many people, fill the void left by the advance of secularization and the alienation from genuine religious traditions so prevalent in the modern world. Ultimate concern gets shown toward wholly inappropriate objects, ranging from the relatively harmless to the dangerous and fatal – from football, through sex, to drugs. Mention has already been made of the secular ideologies like communism and nationalism that have won absolute loyalty and commitment from vast numbers of human beings, with catastrophic consequences. It is remarkable how such ideologies can ape religion – its conversion experiences, its rituals, its charismatic leaders, its characteristic attitudes of devotion, even self-sacrifice.

The prevalence and power of such religion substitutes, while, as I say, bearing witness to certain basic human needs, impress upon us the imperative to define religion proper not just in terms of a particular kind of human attitude or practice, but also in terms of its appropriate object – ultimate reality, the transcendent; in theistic language, God. This marks the difference between idolatry and religion. The problem with idolatry, with the absolutizing of something finite and relative, is the lack of the sense of proportion and the critical distance which men and women need if the values of a humane, tolerant and open society are to be sustained. Admittedly, religion too can become fanatical, especially when allied to some ethnic, nationalist or anti-colonialist cause, but also by itself where commitment is blind and the religious object narrowly or slavishly conceived. That is why it cannot be conceded that any religion will do. Much depends on the breadth of vision and self-critical awareness in terms of which the religious values – the theological virtues of faith, hope and love – are affirmed and lived. And much depends on the nature of the Absolute, the God, believed to be the source and goal of everything. The Christian creed to be examined in this book speaks of the triune God, the God who is love given and received and shared still more, who made the world, who loves all wayward human creatures back into peace with themselves and with their Maker, who indwells the fellowship of the believers, building them up into a serving, worshipping community, and who gathers them into God for ever. Such a God, unlike the cult objects and the objects of religion substitutes, is worthy of worship and of love.

ART AND CULTURE

Great art can itself function as a religion substitute. I am not thinking here so much of the way in which a particular artist's

vocation can become so powerful and absorbing that it over-
rides all ethical commitments and claims, as of the way in
which art, music and culture generally can become, in a relatively harmless way, the sole focus of meaning and value in
people's lives. I have sometimes watched an audience of young
people at a Promenade concert in the Albert Hall listening
with rapt attention to, say, a Bruckner symphony, and breaking out into thunderous applause as the last chords die away,
and found myself reflecting on the virtually religious quality
of their enthusiasm. Similarly, attendance at a truly great
performance of one of Shakespeare's plays, whether history,
comedy or tragedy, can fill one with such a sense of wonder
and terror at the heights and depths and variety of human
existence as they are portrayed in the dramatic interactions
and expressed in the sublime poetry that one can understand
the evident conviction of many people that it is great art
alone that can create and sustain value and significance in
life. The same is true of opera. The combination of music and
drama produces an all-absorbing art form that can be food
and drink to the spirit, as one is caught up in the sheer
creativity and grandeur of the work. As mentioned already, it
is no surprise that many young people choose to study arts
courses rather than the sciences, when daily commerce with
such sublime and beautiful works is on offer.

Certainly, one of the tests of the quality of a civilization is
not only its capacity to foster artistic creativity of the highest
degree, but also its readiness to value the arts and provide
the resources needed to enable them to flourish. The architectural monuments of India or of medieval Europe, the
poetry and drama of Elizabethan England, the musical creativity and life of eighteenth-century Austria, are all examples
of the products of high cultures which, somehow or other,
had it in them not only to elicit such triumphs of the human
spirit, but also to encourage and enable people to find worlds
of meaning in them. Even in relatively philistine and artisti-
cally unproductive ages like our own, at least some resources
are devoted to the preservation and popularization of the
cultural achievements of other places and times.

But these great works of art are most implausibly thought
of as no more than expressions of the human spirit. Equally

implausible is the view that they exist to be enjoyed simply for their own sake. They are indeed intrinsically valuable – beautiful and good – but at the same time and precisely as such they point beyond themselves to the eternal and absolutely beautiful and good. Far from really being a religion substitute, great art is itself a signal of transcendence and a window into eternity.

For one thing, much of the painting, music, literature and architecture that so enhance our lives is religious in inspiration and content. To stand in the Museo Civico in San Sepolcro in Italy and contemplate Piero della Francesca's *The Resurrection* is to share the artist's insight into the transition from creation to new creation about which we shall speak in later chapters of this book. But even where the subject matter of the work of art is not overtly religious, as in the plays of Shakespeare or in many a great novel, the way such works portray the depth and significance of human life, human relationships and human community may readily be taken as revelatory of the image of God in the world – both positively and negatively, the partial fruition of that image, and, of course, its partial loss or distortion. Even Proust's isolated remembrances contain moments of virtually mystical experience. And it has often been pointed out that the music of the brash young Mozart unselfconsciously articulates the harmonies of creation itself.

So art and culture can and should be seen not just as products of human sensibility but as clues to the meaning and worth of the whole cosmic process out of which we have evolved. It is the very nature of aesthetic, as of moral, value that belies materialism as a total world view and provides one of the many starting-points for a cumulative argument for the existence of God.

RECOVERY OF THE SOURCES OF MEANING AND HOPE

Having painted a fairly bleak picture of the modern western world – its loss of a common framework of meaning and purpose, its depersonalizing materialism, its uncontrolled pollution of the planet, the breakdown of its basic moral sense, its irresolvable conflicts at the levels of personal ideal and national aspiration, its tendency towards nihilism – I have begun in the last four sections to point to certain factors on the human scene that may well be thought of as enabling us to resist these self-destructive trends. The riches of history and tradition cannot be so easily dismissed, when the results of that dismissal are experienced as so dire. Religion itself retains its power to meet deep human needs and put people in touch with the dimension of spirituality. At the same time the manifest failure of religion substitutes to provide a genuinely all-embracing and creative philosophy of life drives us back to re-examine the potentialities of the historic faiths for making sense of things and providing resources of meaning and hope. In such contexts, the claims of the moral law get reinforced and undergirded in a way no secular theory can match. And artistic creativity and its life-enhancing products can be seen to point beyond themselves to a transcendent and absolute beauty, glimpsed, as through a glass darkly, in moments of aesthetic rapture.

A cumulative case can be constructed for taking these intimations of divinity and immortality seriously. In the first place, the great world religions offer explanations, not otherwise available, for the very existence of the world. They account, too, for the fact that the basic energies of the cosmos have it in them, over time, to evolve higher and higher forms of life, till consciousness, mind, freedom and reason – the basic constituents of personal and interpersonal life – appear upon the scene. The phenomenon of mind is a much less odd and inexplicable phenomenon if the whole universe out of which it has evolved is itself the product of an absolute, transcendent, mind. Already, of course, at this pretty abstract level, preferences are beginning to be shown for some rather than others of the world religions. Talk of design, purpose and mind already points in the direction of the theistic rather than the non-theistic faiths.

The cumulative case proceeds by dwelling on the factors mentioned in the last few pages – the objectivity of moral values and moral claims, the sheer presence of beauty and creativity in the world. It simply makes more sense to see these things as grounded in absolute goodness and absolute beauty. Their fragile presence in the world is otherwise a complete mystery. To these often-rehearsed springboards of theistic faith may be added the inescapable fact of the objectivity of truth – the fact that we live in a discoverable world, whose nature is not only fixed and given, but rationally intelligible, indeed expressible in mathematical formulae of great elegance and beauty. The sheer givenness of the universe out of which we humans have emerged and which we come to know not only through scientific discovery but also through personal and interpersonal experience, bears mute testimony to the mind of the Maker.

Reference to experience leads us on to what, for many theistic apologists, is the clinching argument in the cumulative case for a return to belief in God: the very fact of religious experience throughout history and all over the world. As already mentioned, this is an extraordinarily widespread phenomenon even in our supposedly secular society – admittedly in pretty strange and sometimes dubious dress. But if there are good reasons for belief in God, it should not surprise us that the human heart is really quite often touched, sometimes against all expectation, by more or less direct intimations of the divine.

All this leaves out of reckoning the question of revelation. But it is not unreasonable to suppose that, if indeed there is an absolute personal source and goal behind and before the whole world process, then that mind and that will would be likely to have made itself known actively and particularly, over and above the universal presence of an all-pervading spirit, of which Wordsworth spoke in his *Lines Composed above Tintern Abbey*. I have already drawn attention to the fact of the great world religions, traditions embracing what have been widely held to be revelations of the divine nature and purpose for the world. Much religious experience is of course coloured and shaped by one or other of these interpretative schemes. But, while the mystical or numinous or devotional experiences of believers within these communities of faith give life and body to religious views of the world, the revelation claims themselves, handed down in scriptures and creeds and confessions, and reflected on and articulated in the various theologies of the theistic religions, give content and a comprehensive vision to the ways in which God, the universe and humankind are experienced and understood. Revelation also gives particular content to both personal and communal ideals of life, towards which, through the resources of the spirit, people are enabled to work. It is the truth content of one such revelation claim that is to be explored and defended in this book.

THE PHENOMENON OF CHRISTIANITY

Among the data thrown up, as it were, by the history of religions, is Christianity – by any reckoning a remarkable phenomenon on the world scene. It is still, in so far as such figures can be gathered, the largest in numbers of the great world religions. The current *Encyclopedia Britannica Yearbook* (1996) lists adherents to Christianity as numbering some 1,928 million out of a world population of 5,716 million. (The next largest religion is Islam, with some 1,099 million adherents.) The regions with the largest number of Christians are Latin America and Africa, and these are well known to be the areas of most rapid growth. Of the 1,928 million, 968 million are Roman Catholic, 396 million Protestant, 218 million Orthodox, 71 million Anglican, and 276 million 'other'.

Christianity is approaching its third millennium. It began as a Jewish sect in ancient Palestine, and spread from the middle east westwards, largely through the communication system and political framework of the Roman Empire. At first a persecuted sect, its rapid spread led to its adoption as the Roman Empire's official religion in the early fourth century. Many of its greatest thinkers came from outside Europe – Egypt, Syria and North Africa – and despite the great influence of Rome and the early Papacy, the Councils that formulated the so-called Nicene Creed, which is to be the focus of our exposition of classical Christianity in this book, took place in Asia Minor. But, despite ancient forays into south India, and the preservation of small ancient Churches in the middle east, Christianity was largely a European phenomenon for over a thousand years. This was chiefly due to the spread of Islam through the middle east and North Africa and the consequent loss of most of the ancient eastern centres of early Christianity, including Constantinople. There were Roman Catholic missions to the far east in the seventeenth century and Puritan migrations to the New World at about the same time. Christianity soon became an important factor in the United States, north and south, and, of course, in Australia. But the nineteenth century was the great century of missionary expansion world-wide. Christianity is indeed a world religion, with huge and growing numbers in Africa and Latin America as already pointed out, significant minorities in the Indian subcontinent, South-East Asia (notably the Philippines) and the far east, and very small minorities in most Muslim lands. But the Roman Catholic Church, the Anglican Communion and the other member Churches of the World Council of Churches, in their different ways, constitute genuinely international bodies, with world-wide representation and influence.

All these Christian people and Christian churches subscribe to the Nicene Creed. (We shall in due course consider – with some sympathy – why the Eastern Orthodox Churches quarrel with one small clause of it.) The faith summed up in the creeds is what these people live by and what motivates and energizes their worship, their communal life, their commitments to making the world a better place, and their hopes for the future. The substance of that faith – trust in the God they believe to have made the world, and to have revealed his life-transforming love by entering it, winning his creatures' response and renewing their own life and love for all eternity – is the object of our enquiry here. Is it really true?

THE CREEDS AND THE BIBLE IN TODAY'S WORLD

A word should be said at the end of this introductory chapter on why it is one of the historic creeds rather than the Bible that is to be the focus of our enquiry. After all, it is the Bible, not the creeds, that is holy Scripture for Christians. The supposed revelation to which Christianity is the response is surely more immediately accessible in the words of Scripture rather than in later summaries, hammered out by argumentative bishops in council.

Certainly the books of the Bible are the primary witnesses to divine revelation, and, used wisely in both preaching and private study, they can indeed *become* the Word of God to us today. But, all the same, the Bible consists of a very mixed and unsystematic collection of witnesses. The Old Testament, so Christians believe, points forward to the coming of Jesus Christ and reflects, therefore, the faith and understanding of the people chosen to provide the context for the incarnation. It does so, partly, in story form, recounting the history through which Israel's faith was formed and developed. It does so partly through law codes, prophetic oracles and wisdom sayings, all, in their differing ways, giving expression to the people's understanding of the nature, will and purpose of their God. The New Testament records the story of Jesus, his teaching, his fate and its aftermath, from a variety of perspectives, and goes on to present a short narrative of the growth of the earliest Christian communities, supplemented by a collection of occasional letters, reflecting both permanent insights into the meaning of the whole Christ event, and also particular disputes and problems that arose in those early days of the formation and nurture of the small Christian communities between Jerusalem and Rome. It ends with an extraordinary visionary prophecy, allegedly unveiling the heavenly realm and foretelling the winding up of all things in God's plan.

All this is indispensable. It puts us in touch with what God has done to make himself known and rescue his people – not only the Jews, but the whole human race – from their lost and alienated condition. But it is not in itself revelation. Christians do not regard the Bible in the way Muslims regard the Qur'an, as God's own dictation. The various books of the Old and New Testaments, in themselves, are human testimonies and responses to God's acts in history. They become the Word of God to individuals and congregations in so far as they enable faith and open people's eyes to what God has done, is doing and intends. But that does not prevent them containing, in themselves, much all-too-human, fallible, material. And in no way are they systematic treatises, spelling out, or even summing up, the essence of Christianity.

The Bible, therefore, can at best be held to contain the raw material of Christian theology, and it is no wonder that the early Christian leaders turned to philosophy to help them tease out the meaning of the faith into which they had been drawn. There were pros and cons, of course, in that whole process; and in the twentieth century we have become more aware of the problematic aspects of that philosophical influence. But that some systematic reflection on the significance of the events recorded in the Bible was a necessary step can hardly be doubted. And if biblical faith is to be appropriated in the late twentieth century, the same process of distilling the essence of the story and relating it to everything else must take place today.

But we cannot just go direct to the Bible. Christianity would not be the same thing at all if the Scriptures had been lost entirely, the story forgotten, and then the Bible rediscovered afresh two thousand years later. The events to which the Bible bears witness had an immediate effect in the birth of a community of faith with which we stand in relations of continuity. That community and its self-understanding became part of the faith itself. So the first agreed distillations of the content of the biblical faith – the creeds of the undivided Church – have a classic place and an indispensable role in the articulations of what Christianity is for today.

CHAPTER TWO

Belief in God

THEISM AND ATHEISM

The Nicene Creed begins with the unqualified affirmation that we – that is, the Christians, both as individuals and as the Church – believe in one God. What does this mean? It means that Christians are not atheists, denying the existence of God. Nor are they agnostics, uncertain whether or not there is a God. Christians are theists. ('Theist' means one who believes in God.) Moreover, Christians are monotheists, like Jews and Muslims and many others, denying the existence of many gods. That is why they spell 'God' with a capital 'G' and keep resolutely to the singular. Only when speaking of polytheism – belief in many gods – do they resort to a lower case 'g', and clearly they suppose that gods in that sense do not exist. At best such gods are poorly understood person-ifications of aspects of the one true God. At worst they are fictions.

But what does the word 'God' mean? What are Christians, like other theists, talking about when they thus distinguish themselves from atheists and agnostics? Like any other word, the word 'God' has a long history; and part of that history is the refinement away from generic uses characteristic of polytheism, where gods were superior, but finite, spiritual beings behind the great forces of nature or the state, and towards its singular, absolute, capital 'G' use, where 'God' means the infinite, yet personal, source, ground and goal of the whole cosmos. This refinement took place at varying stages in the history of religions, and in varying ways, in the Indian subcontinent, for example, and in the middle east.

There – in the middle east – the religions of semitic origin, Judaism, Christianity and Islam, refined this absolute understanding of God into particularly powerful strands of ethical monotheism.

It sometimes seems as if 'God' with a capital 'G' functions as a name. Christians in their prayers and worship address their maker, their redeemer and the spiritual energizer of their life together, as 'God'. But the word 'God' is not really a name. As many have pointed out, it is translated into other languages, and even in its refined uses carries primarily a descriptive sense, spelled out in terms like 'creator', 'spirit' and 'lord', and qualified by adjectives like 'almighty', 'infinite', 'transcendent' and 'immanent', whose meaning we shall need to explore as we try to tease out the sense of what it is to believe in God. God *is* addressed by name. The Jews, though with the greatest reticence, know God by the name of Jahweh. The Muslims, much more confidently, refer to God as Allah. Curiously the Christians, though, of course, they know their incarnate God by his human, given name of Jesus, are much less inclined to give God, as such, a name. In the next chapter we shall be exploring the specifically Christian understanding of God as the blessed Trinity, but God the Father, God the Son and God the Holy Spirit are still addressed and referred to chiefly in descriptive language, not by name.

There is another way of approaching the meaning of the word 'God', though this too goes better with the lower case, generic use, namely by noting the way people sometimes speak of what most concerns them as their 'god'. As already pointed out, for some people, money, or sport, or even their car is their 'god'. But this subjective approach trivializes the issue. True, the God religion knows is, or ought to be, the object of ultimate concern; but the whole point of religious belief is lost if it is defined solely in terms of human attitudes and commitments. What matters, in the great historical religious traditions like Christianity, is that there is found to be, beyond, behind, or within the everyday world, and indeed the whole physical cosmos, an absolute and ultimate Reality, worthy of trust, worthy of worship and active in evoking both belief and commitment.

So to believe in God is to accept that the everyday world in which we find ourselves, and which science explores and understands in ever-increasing detail and comprehensiveness, is neither self-explanatory nor just a brute fact. It is a meaningful universe just because it depends for its being, its nature and its destiny, on an infinite, all-encompassing and all-pervading spiritual source, ground and goal.

IS GOD REAL?

There is a recurring tendency in the modern world not simply to deny the reality of God in the objective, 'metaphysical', sense just outlined, but to retain the full use of the word 'God' for other purposes. Whereas people used – as many indeed still do – to think of themselves as agnostics or atheists where the question of God is concerned, there are an increasing number of basically religious people – 'religious' in the subjective though non-trivial sense of manifesting certain all-embracing feelings, attitudes and policies of life – who find themselves unable to believe in the objective reality of God, but who do not wish to abandon 'God-talk' altogether. Rather, they wish to go on using the word 'God' purely symbolically, as shorthand for their unqualified ideals or commitments; ideals and commitments inherited from the great religions but now, they think, best detached from the old framework of belief in an objective, transcendent yet immanent, spiritual reality 'beyond' the physical cosmos and the merely human world. The whole language of religion, spirituality and worship gets taken over for the articulation and reinforcement of certain fundamentally ethical, communal, all-embracing, life-ways.

There is no denying the sincerity of those who wish to use religious language this way, and their ideals are certainly worthy of respect. But there is equally no denying the completeness of the break with traditional religion that this way of using religious language involves. The essence of Christianity – certainly the Christianity of the Bible and the creeds, but also the Christianity of the vast majority of living Christians, including the vast majority of contemporary theologians and philosophers of religion – is inescapably bound up with belief in the objective reality of God. And to translate

God-talk out of this context of metaphysical realism is to offer one of those interpretations mentioned in the introduction that can only be regarded as beyond the pale. There is no way in which any of the Christian Churches could ever be expected to endorse this subjectivist, purely human, interpretation of the Christian creeds, even as one of a wide range of permissible interpretations.

This judgement is not just a historical or sociological comment, still less the expression of a conservative opinion. It reflects the fact that Christianity is, essentially, bound up with the truth of belief in the objective reality of God. So it is worth while reminding ourselves right at the start of this exposition of the doctrines of the Creed, why it is that objective theism is held, not only by the present author, but by all the Christian Churches, to be essential, indeed, fundamental, to the Christian faith. In brief, the truth of objective theism is vouched for by a combination of reason, experience and revelation.

Reason, as indicated in chapter one, still seeks the best explanation for the world's existence and its capacity to produce life, mind, goodness and beauty. Non-objective God-talk is no better placed than straight atheism or frank agnosticism to explain these basic facts of our world and our experience. Religious experience too, in its many different guises, is hard to account for in naturalistic or purely humanist terms. So often the human spirit is encountered, energized, or transformed by a spiritual power or resource from beyond. Even where, as is often the case, the divine call or inspiration wells up from within a person's own heart, mind or spirit, it strikes the recipient as something not of his own making, something beyond her own natural capacities. And, as we shall see, these rational and experiential intimations are given all-encompassing interpretation by traditions based on powerful revelation claims. Indeed it is the inner rationality of the revelation-based world view handed down in credal Christianity that is being explored in these pages. That world view, from the very start, involves the objective reality of God, as creator, revealer and redeemer of the world.

THE OTHERNESS OF GOD

All this entails that Christians are no more pantheists than they are agnostics, atheists or polytheists. Pantheism – the belief that the whole world is God – shares with the mono-theistic faiths the view that materialistic naturalism makes little sense. But the idea that God and the world are different aspects or expressions of the one, same, fundamental reality does not begin to do justice to the conviction of the other-ness of God found at the heart of Judaism, Christianity and Islam. This will be clear when we expound the doctrine of creation; for the Creator/creature distinction is of the essence of credal Christianity. This is the point at which the rational considerations mentioned in the last section tell against pantheism and in favour of theism. Pantheism lacks theism's explanatory force.

At the same time, the experiential factors – of awe, wor-ship, inspiration and vocation – all tell against pantheistic identity of ourselves, our world and God, and in favour of the relational view of the world's and our dependence on God as our Creator and our Lord. And this God/world distinction is only reinforced by the revelatory factors to be discussed in the next section – the disclosures, that is, from the side of God that there is indeed a transcendent origin, purpose, meaning and goal to the whole world process and to individual human lives.

The otherness of God is summed up in this notion of tran-scendence. Our finite, contingent, non-self-explanatory world points beyond itself, beyond everything that science unpacks about its inbuilt laws and given powers, to an absolute, infi-nite, genuinely self-explanatory ground. This transcendent, all-encompassing world ground is, admittedly, in some cul-tures and some religions, thought of in impersonal terms. But that fails to account for the purpose, the intention, the will, and, as Christians particularly see it, the love that lie behind the world process and the human story. These personal attrib-utes of God the Creator raise great problems concerning the presence of so much evil and suffering in the world, and we shall have to consider these problems in our reflections on creation in chapter four. But there is just too much requiring

explanation in terms of will, too much pointing to some ultimate personal encounter, too much bespeaking self-revelation
of an active purpose at the heart of things, for Christians to
permit themselves to fall back on the idea of an impersonal
transcendence. Talk of God's transcendence must, of course,
be matched by talk of the divine immanence – God's
omnipresence, indwelling and pervading the whole created
cosmos. As we shall see, it is a grave error to think of the
universe as posited in being and left to its own devices to
evolve worlds of life entirely under its own steam. The transcendent Creator Spirit is present and active in, with and
under every facet of the world process, not least in the human
heart and soul, where God is experienced and known to be
closer than breathing, welling up from within. But this immanence of God does not belie God's otherness. The indwelling
Spirit is no more to be identified with some worldly or purely
human reality than is the transcendent creative energy that
lies behind and beyond the whole world. Neither as transcendent nor as immanent is God the same thing as the world
deep down.

   If Christianity is to be distinguished from pantheism and
impersonal transcendence as well as from polytheism, atheism
and agnosticism, there is another view, known as 'panentheism', to which a number of Christian scholars – this would
hardly be ascribed to ordinary Christians in the pew – have
been, perhaps more reasonably, attracted. Panentheism is the
view that everything – the physical universe and ourselves –
exists in God. From within his own infinite substance God
fashions a contingent universe out of which to evolve worlds
of life and spirit. On this view, God and the world are not
distinct, externally related, realities. The world is not created
'out of nothing' as, for the most part, Christian tradition has
held (on this see chapter four), but rather the whole creative
process is a kind of self-projection of the divine, bringing
about the conditions under which finite persons can come to
be and to relate to each other and to God, enjoying a kind of
relative autonomy within the divine life, and destined, so
some have suggested, to be absorbed back into the infinite in
the end. This view could, I think, be classed as falling within
the range of permissible options for a Christian doctrine of

God. But we shall see reason to remain somewhat suspicious of panentheism. There is still a tendency here to bring the reality of God within an overall conceptual scheme that fails to do justice to the otherness and 'prior actuality' of God. We shall be returning to this question in chapters three and four.

GOD'S SELF-REVELATION

It has already been pointed out that rational and experiential indications and intimations of the reality of God find confirmation in God's own active self-revelation. The being, the nature and the will of God are conveyed to humankind, not directly out of the blue, but indirectly, through thoroughly human media. Two factors should incline us to be cautious in speaking of God's self-revelation. One is this matter of the all-too-human mediation of divine revelation; the other is the unavoidable *mystery* of the infinite and absolute reality we call 'God'. There is, necessarily, a sense in which God remains hidden even in his self-revelation. But there is also a sense in which God does make himself *known* through the founders, prophets, gurus and scriptures of the great religions and through what they bear witness to.

This talk of human mediation of divine self-revelation shows that we are thinking here of the special revelations that have been given over and above any general revelation that may occur through nature, through conscience and through religious experience all over the world. Many people, not only the Psalmist, have held that 'the heavens tell out the glory of God'. Many, not only Matthew Arnold, have sensed 'a power, not ourselves, that makes for righteousness'. And many, in very different times, places and cultures have experienced 'numinous' awe or mystical ecstasy. But, as one might expect if God is real, there are many, more specific, forms of alleged divine self-disclosure to be reckoned with in human history, and especially in and through the history of religions.

I write in this pretty general way about special revelations in the plural, partly because it makes little sense to suppose that the God of the whole earth will have restricted self-disclosure of his nature and will to a single strand of human history, and partly because the actual content of the history of

religions, as well as manifesting striking differences, also
shows remarkable common features in the spirituality, the
worship and the transformative power evoked by different
traditions of theistic faith. It is an implication of what has
been said so far that it must be one and the same God who
not only is glimpsed and experienced in different ways
world-wide, but also is active in fashioning special channels
of spiritual growth and transformation throughout human
history in all parts of the globe. And certainly the religions of
semitic origin are bound to admit that Yahweh and the God
and Father of our Lord Jesus Christ and Allah are, ultimately
speaking, one and the same, self-revealing, God.

Even so, it is hard for any of these faiths to rest content with
an unqualified pluralism in these matters. We have already
seen reason to prefer the strands of personal monotheism to
those of impersonal monism in world religion. And while
Jews, Christians and Muslims should be happy to affirm
divine self-revelation in the more cosmic, ahistorical, religions
of the east, they are bound to accord greater world-historical
significance to the self-disclosure of God which they believe
to have taken place in and through a particular sequence of
historical events and a particular growing tradition of faith
and understanding. For they discern a rationale, a providential
intelligibility, in the idea of gradual, progressive, revelation,
creative of a people of God intended to be a light to the
nations and a special witness to the nature and will of God for
the whole Earth. They also hold that this particular story has
enabled them to see world history in linear, progressive,
terms as having a hidden thread, leading in a particular direction and pointing to a single, final, destiny for the whole
human story in the end.

It is, of course, a huge difficulty for this way of looking at
things (which we owe to the religions of semitic origin) that
they themselves have come to construe this one history of
humanly mediated divine self-revelation so very differently.
For the Jews, the Hebrew Bible bears witness to divine revelation in the giving of God's law, in the songs and proverbs of
the Wisdom tradition, and in the prophetic oracles and
reflections on Israel's often tortuous history. For the
Christians, all this is indeed affirmed as divine revelation, but

believed to reach its providential culmination in the coming
of the Christ, in a human life-story held to incarnate God's
very presence in person in our midst. For the Muslims, however, Jesus is but one of a series of inspired prophets, a line
which reaches its climax in Muhammad, to whom God is held
to have dictated his final revelation, the Qur'an – the very
words of God to humankind.

It is up to our Jewish and Muslim friends to tell the story
from their own perspective and to spell out its inner rationale
and religious plausibility in relation to everything else. Here
we shall be setting out the Christian understanding of God's
special self-revelation. As stressed already, this means reflection not so much on the Bible – for Christians do not identify
the Bible with revelation just like that – as on the events culminating in the incarnation and its consequences, to which
the Scriptures bear their variegated human witness. To repeat
– the creeds sum up the truth content believed by Christians
to emerge from reflection on that story.

As we shall see, it is the central conviction of the Christian
Church that God's self-revelation reached a unique and unre-
peatable climax in the incarnation – the coming in human
form of God himself in one of the modes of his eternal being,
in order to enact and manifest the divine love in person and
to win God's wayward creatures into a fuller, deeper, life and
fellowship in God. This is what makes religious pluralism –
the view that all religions are equally profound and equally
successful channels of divine/human encounter – impossible
for Christians plausibly to hold.

GOD THE FATHER

I return, then, to the understanding of God that finds
expression in the Christian creeds. And immediately we
encounter the fact that in the Christian tradition, as already
in ancient Israel, God is referred to and addressed as 'Father'.
This usage, reflected and endorsed as it is in the first clause
of the Lord's Prayer, sums up several central and essential
facets of the Christian understanding of God. It expresses the
unequivocally personal nature of Christian theism, to which
attention has already been drawn. It expresses something of

the relation of origination in which God stands towards all his human creatures. And above all it captures something of the oversight, care, concern and steadfast love that God is believed to exercise towards his 'children'. In Christian theism, of course, a certain withdrawal occurs from identifying God *tout court* as Father. God the Father comes to be thought of as but one mode or personal centre in God and identified as the first Person of the Trinity. We shall consider what this means in the next chapter. But, clearly, trinitarian belief is initially expressed by positing something analogous to a father/son relation in God.

Ignoring for the moment this trinitarian aspect of talk of the fatherhood of God, let us press the question whether we are simply speaking metaphorically of God when we address him as 'Father'. Most of the language we use in speaking of God, and certainly all the personal terms we use, get their meaning initially in the context of human life and experience, and then get refined and qualified when transferred to talk of the transcendent. We shall look at some of these qualifications shortly. But a degree of anthropomorphism in our talk of God is inevitable. This does not mean that we are projecting the idea of God after our own image. On the contrary, the Judaeo-Christian tradition has always taught that we humans are made in the image of God, that key features of human existence – our reason, our freedom, our will, our personhood, our love – mirror and were intended to mirror central features of the divine life. These attributes are more than mere metaphors. It is true that in us they exist in a finite, embodied form. But this fact does not belong to the essence of these attributes. In God they exist in an infinite, incorporeal, purely spiritual mode and are thus the perfect, supreme, exemplars of what is meant by reason, freedom, will, personhood and love.

But what about the fatherhood of God? Well, it is clear that fatherhood is more closely tied down to finite, embodied, human life than are the more universal personal attributes just mentioned. We have to think away all biological aspects of human parenthood, when we call God our Father. Equally, we have to think away all sexual and gender connotations when we think of or address our heavenly Father. The infinite

Spirit beyond and at the heart of things is obviously neither
male nor female; for sex and gender are aspects of finite,
embodied, life. For this very reason, it is quite permissible, at
times, to speak of the motherhood of God; for there may be
some features of parental care and love more often associated
with the mother which, in prayer and worship, can be
employed, in an exalted, transferred, sense, in talk of God.
But this is the point. What differentiates 'father' and 'mother'
from 'person', 'will', 'mind' and 'love' is that, while the latter
group can be applied directly, albeit analogically, to God, the
former two are only appropriate in certain respects. More
work has to be done to free them from their finite, biological,
sexual, context and to allow the aspects of parental care and
love appropriate in talk of God to carry the intended meaning.

We have still not finished with the problems felt in the
modern world by talk of the fatherhood of God. Even when
it is realized that such talk carries no connotations of embodiment, still less of sexuality, it may still be felt that such talk
comes down to us from a patriarchal society with an inbuilt
tendency to reinforce attitudes of male dominance in ways we
wish to distance ourselves from today. I have some sympathy
with those who, for this reason, make the decision to avoid
not only the term 'father' but also the masculine pronoun,
'he', in talk of God, and simply to repeat the word 'God' and
the possessive, 'God's', in worship and theology alike.

If, nevertheless, I do not endorse that decision or follow
that practice here, it is not just for stylistic reasons or because
I do not wish to cut myself off from the literature and the
traditional liturgical texts of my religion. The fact is that talk
of God as our Father is too deeply ingrained in the Judaeo-
Christian tradition – a tradition itself regarded as providential in the purposes of God – and too central to the teaching
of Jesus, whom Christians believe to be (in a sense yet to be
unpacked) God incarnate, for the Church to feel free to make
such a radical break. After all, if we can free ourselves from
biological and sexual implications when we call God our
Father, we can also free ourselves from the ideas of male
dominance and any other undesirable and inappropriate
connotations that the idea of fatherhood may happen to
carry with it. When Jesus taught his disciples to pray, 'Our

Father . . .', the aspects of parental care and love intended to be conveyed – as seen from the rest of the prayer – have no more to do with male dominance than they do with masculinity or biological parenting. And the Lord's Prayer should function as the Church's yardstick in interpreting the Creed's first clause: 'We believe in one God, the Father . . .'.

THE ALMIGHTY

Older translations of the Nicene Creed have a single phrase, 'the Father Almighty', in apposition to 'one God'. The modern agreed version puts 'the Almighty' as a separate, second, explanatory phrase. In doing so, it goes back to the early biblical roots of the credal doctrine of God, where God is certainly addressed as 'Father' and characterized as 'Almighty' (indeed 'El Shaddai' – 'the Almighty' – was one of the names of God in the Hebrew Bible), but never together, with the adjective 'almighty' qualifying 'Father'.

The new translation is certainly an improvement. Partly it reflects the trinitarian structure of the Creed, the first main paragraph referring to the first Person of the Trinity, God the Father, and therefore requiring separate affirmation of belief in the Father, as later in the Son and in the Spirit. And partly it reflects the need to allow the phrase, 'the Almighty', like 'Creator' which follows, to stand in apposition not only to 'the Father' but to 'one God'. For although the Christian tradition has tended to associate the divine sovereignty and the divine creativity particularly with the first Person of the Trinity, these attributes are also quite properly associated with the one God in all the modes of his being.

The first thing that the phrase 'the Almighty' conveys is indeed God's sovereignty over the whole of creation. It is quite natural that any form of pure ethical monotheism will recognize and affirm God's universal lordship over all that he has made. This aspect of Jewish faith is held in common by the Muslims as well as by the Christians. But already in the Hebrew Bible, ideas of God's patience and God's love were prevailing over those of God's kingly rule. And in the New Testament, the discernment of God's power in the weakness

of Christ's cross led to far-reaching, even paradoxical, qualifications to the Christian understanding of omnipotence. True,
God is the God who raises the dead. This aspect of God's sovereignty is central to the Christian gospel. That God's way is
not that of brute force and overweening power, but rather
that of grace and love, is one of the main ways in which the
more obvious sense of God's power over all things gets
refined and spiritualized in Christianity.

This is just as well, since notions such as sovereignty, lordship and kingship undoubtedly have historical and cultural
connotations with ancient forms of monarchy and absolute
rule, from which the followers of Jesus Christ are bound to
wish to distance themselves, not least in an egalitarian, democratic, culture such as ours. But it needs to be stressed that it
is not principally modern democratic notions that require of
Christianity some revision of the natural picture of God's
power. It is the New Testament's witness to the way of the
cross and to the love of God that impose this re-evaluation on
the Church, age after age.

Many people in the modern western world have reacted
very strongly against the idea of a supreme divine monarch.
God's power is widely felt to infringe human freedom and sti-
fle human creativity. But this reaction is to a mistaken, albeit
natural, picture of God. The God revealed in Jesus Christ is
one who lets his creatures be, respects their freedom, and
draws them into relation with each other and with himself,
only by grace and love.

God, on the Christian understanding, is indeed omnipotent. His power is infinite. No other being can have power
over God, except by God's own patience and restraint.
'Omnipotent' is one of the qualifiers by which we free ourselves from anthropomorphic, all-too-human, analogies in our
talk of God. But, clearly, what God can do and does do must
be consistent with his nature. God cannot contradict himself.
He cannot do evil. And if, in the creation of a world of finite
life, of derived creativity and of creaturely inter-subjectivity,
he limits himself to the ways of patience, grace and love, that
reflects no lack of power, but rather exemplifies the divine
omnipotence. For, out of his great love, the Lord of all lets us

be and wins our response without force. In the end, so
Christians believe, he will bring his creative project to a perfect consummation. But there are no short cuts to the
'kingdom' of God. I shall return to this question of God's self-
limitation and necessary self-restraint when I come to consider the problem of evil in chapter four.

THE CREATOR

The most basic identifying description of God in all the
monotheistic faiths is that which speaks of God as 'Creator',
'maker of heaven and earth'. What it means to see this world
– this whole universe – as 'creation' will be set out and
explored in chapter four. Here we are considering the divine
side of the God/world relation – God's act of positing the
world in being. When a child asks, 'Who made the world?', or
'Where does the world come from?', the immediate religious
answer is, 'God made the world'. The child may, of course, go
on to ask, 'Who made God?', but that really is a child's question, since, in the monotheistic faiths, it is precisely because
the world is held to require explanation – the existence of
matter or energy, possessing very specific powers and operating under very specific fundamental laws being, as far as
we can see, non-self-explanatory – that an absolute, infinite,
self-explanatory ground and origin is affirmed. As already
stressed, the quest for the best explanation of the world's
existence leads to the supposition of an infinite Creator quite
other than the world. It was this, more than anything, that
rendered atheism and non-realist God-talk alike highly
implausible.
     God's making of the world is, of course, an analogical
notion. Pictures are drawn, quite naturally, from human creativity. All the models are of intentional activity – a purposive
explanation being held to render the effect more intelligible
than a non-purposive origin. But some models are more inadequate than others. We cannot go far with analogies from
human crafts. The potter's intention and activity may explain
the pot; but the existence of the clay is presupposed. And,
in any case, a pot is a poor analogy for a world of free and

rational persons. Artistic creativity is perhaps a better model. A great composer brings into being something genuinely new. Much has been made of the drama of creation – the characters, the plot, the complex, deep interrelationships, with elements of both comedy and tragedy. Novels and operas furnish similar fruitful models, well worth pondering and developing. But nothing in our own experience really compares with the sheer positing and holding in being of an evolving physical universe, productive of self-conscious, rational, free and interactive persons, whose story unfolds, not in a pre-ordained, deterministic way, but under the guidance of a providence that respects and interacts with our freedom.

God is described in this first main paragraph of the Creed as 'maker of heaven and earth'. That may reflect an outmoded cosmology; and we can quite easily read it as meaning, simply, the whole evolving cosmos. Alternatively, we can take 'heaven' to mean the higher spheres of God's creation – the equally created realm of the angels, if there are such, and of the blessed dead. Reasons will be given, in chapter four, for some wariness about the existence of angels, but, on any Christian view, God's creation involves more than the evolving physical universe that has produced us through cosmic and biological evolution. The God who raises the dead, so Christians believe, is fashioning a new creation out of the old and raising those formed on earth to an imperishable eternal future. That final consummation, about which more will be said in chapter ten, is still creation, still posited and held in being by God, the maker of all things.

When the Creed goes on to speak of God as maker 'of all that is, seen and unseen', it is not simply repeating itself; for there are unseen aspects of the present phase of God's creative process, to which religion is better attuned than is a secular, empirical, attitude that restricts itself to what the senses yield. Of course the human senses only put us in touch with a very restricted range of aspects of the physical cosmos. There is much that is 'unseen' about the universe that science probes. But the Creed is more concerned here with the 'unseen' world of the spirit, dimensions of the cosmos that themselves transcend or escape the various nets of scientific enquiry. We shall refer to these dimensions of creation in the course of chapter four.

OTHER ATTRIBUTES OF GOD

There are many other attributes of God not mentioned in the Creed. Omnipotence is only one of the qualifiers which we have to apply to the models of God as Father, Creator and Lord. As already intimated, all finite, limited analogies have to be refined and extended in the direction of the transcendent, if they are to characterize the infinite, absolute, source and will behind everything.

God is omniscient. He knows all things; he knows, that is, everything that can be known, and all the possibilities inherent in what he is making and doing. Doubts have quite reasonably been expressed about God's knowledge of the precise future, if that future is open and not yet decided by those to whom the gift of freedom has been given. This too will be explored further in chapter four. God is omnipresent. The creative activity of God embraces and encompasses the whole creation as it unfolds and develops within God's providence. And God is unchanging in the sense that his core attributes persist – the same yesterday, today and for ever.

God is eternal, not necessarily in the sense of the static timelessness which we associate with Plato's Forms, but in the sense of being everlasting, free from decay and the kind of change that characterizes our space/time world. God is not part of, or limited to, the space/time structure of creation. God's time is deeper, primordial, unaffected by relativity or thermodynamics. The suspicion that the philosophy of Plato came to influence the development of Christian doctrine in the early centuries far too much has led to the kind of questioning of traditional views of divine immutability and timelessness illustrated by the above remarks. It has led some to speak of God's own history and of the story of creation being taken into God's own time. It is in this connection that talk of the creation of an open-futured world, entailing divine ignorance of precisely what is going to happen, makes sense; indeed, makes more sense than the supposition that the whole story of creation, past, present and future, is known all at once to the timeless divine omniscience. In any event, here is an area in the Christian understanding of God where a diversity of views, and some considerable revision of classical Christian doctrine, is a real and quite permissible possibility. I will not, however, call into question divine incorporeality. Everything that has been said about the infinity and 'prior actuality' of the Creator goes against the idea of the world as God's body. God is spirit, necessary and indivisible. Matter is finite, contingent and divisible. Indeed, organic matter as we know it is corruptible, inevitably subject to decay into patterns of energy at the opposite extreme to personal life and cultural innovation. Even if, in the new creation, the resurrection 'body' and the resurrection 'world' are made incorruptible and immortal, they are still finite, dependent, created realities, not aspects of God's own being and nature. Here the tradition stands firm.

THE LOVE OF GOD

Of all the divine attributes not explicitly mentioned in the Creed, the most central and important is that of God's love. Indeed, God *is* love, according to St John. Much more will have to be said about this in the next chapter; for, while many religions speak of God's love for the world, only Christianity has developed the idea that in God there is love given and love received, and love shared still more. It is this trinitarian understanding of God that enables Christians to say that God's love does not depend on there being a created world for God to have an object of his love. There are eternal subject/object relations of love in God.

Nevertheless, it is, of course, believed by Christians that the God, who is love, loves his 'children' – the creatures made in God's image, with whom, at great cost to himself, he identifies in the person of Jesus Christ and whom he draws into loving relation to each other and himself. For although the Creed does not explicitly mention the love of God, the story of our redemption, summarized in the second main paragraph of the Creed and explored here in chapters five and six, is the story of what God did, out of his great love, to redeem and immortalize his wayward human creatures. And we have already had cause to insist that all the attributes of God that constitute his maximal greatness have in their turn to be qualified and reinterpreted in terms of God's active grace and love.

Many people, in the face of the untold suffering and evil that the world contains, remain unconvinced by Christian talk of the love of God. That is why, in the chapter on creation, I shall have to deal with the problem of evil and try to show why it is that the Creator Spirit has to respect the structures of his creation and the freedom of humans, if the intended purpose of fashioning a free communion of loving creatures is to be achieved. And much more will have to be said in the subsequent chapters about the way in which the love of God manifests itself and takes effect in the created world.

THE HIDDENNESS OF GOD

Something should perhaps be inserted at this point about the fact, mentioned earlier, that God remains hidden even in the revelation of the divine love. I am not referring here to the blinkered, the worldly or the secular-minded, for whom God is unquestionably hidden. I have in mind, rather, the many people on the fringes of religion and the Church – and indeed many self-confessed Christians, too – who, for much of the time, sense only the absence of God, whose awareness of the reality of God, let alone the love of God, is fragile and sporadic at best. There are many factors accounting for this elusiveness. One is certainly the problem of evil; and part of our account of why God permits so much to go wrong in the world and in people's lives will involve attempting to show the wider necessities of indirect communication. It is again a question of the otherness of God. God is not a part of, or an element in, the world, to be detected by the means we use to identify and interact with worldly realities. We shall be arguing that a regularly structured, evolving, universe is a necessary condition for the emergence and growth of finite personal life; and, by the same token, God is bound to act and make himself known indirectly, in and through created media, not least the human heart. It should not surprise us that the reality and love of God take some discernment. Spiritual preparation and spiritual training are, in most cases, necessary conditions of spiritual perception.

These necessities are all the more urgent in a secular age. As mentioned in chapter one, social conditioning can work either way. In the so-called ages of faith, it was much easier for people to recognize God as the ultimate, ever-present, context of their lives. This was true, even where life was much harsher than it is today, at least in the developed countries. Now, the secular, science-based, attitudes characteristic of much westernized existence militate against recognition of the spiritual dimension and of God as the ground and goal of everything. To become aware of the presence of God and of the love of God, and to hear the voice of God in vocation, conscience and succour, is to swim against the tide.

EXPERIENCE OF GOD

Nevertheless, experience of God, in very diverse modes, is widely reported, even in the west. As urged before, this is a central facet of religion world-wide. Restricting ourselves here to the Christian context, we need to reckon with the fact that the beliefs summarized in the Christian creeds are never matters solely of the intellect. One way or another, they are given cash value in the varieties of Christian experience.

It is a mistake to think only of the most striking forms of Christian experience, like the overpowering sense of union with God or with Christ that we read of in the writings of great mystics like St John of the Cross or Dame Julian of Norwich. Nor is it right to suppose that devotional ecstasy or a continuous vivid sense of living in the presence of God are at all common even amongst professed Christians. Outbreaks of charismatic experience – people allegedly being taken out of themselves in the Spirit, perhaps even speaking in tongues – are often cited nowadays as evidence of God at work in people's lives; but these manifestations are at best another, relatively rare, mode of extremely vivid Christian experience, and at worst a distraction from the supremely personal and rational nature of the God who is both love and wisdom and, as we shall see, the source of the Spirit's gifts of fellowship, discernment and love.

There are, in all Christians' lives, moments of ecstasy and deep joy and moments of inspiration that have some kinship with the more exalted states just mentioned. But for most Christians most of the time, experience of God is mediated more prosaically through the regular worship of the Church and through practices of prayer and contemplation very far from easy to sustain. As already mentioned, Christian people are, mostly, more aware of God through being sustained in times of difficulty, being convicted by their consciences, whether of what they have done wrong or of the right they know they must perform, or being touched – occasionally overwhelmed – by feelings of wonder or gratitude.

The more exalted states can be a source of pride and division. If so, they have very little to do with the God of the Christians. For example, just as none of the great mystics for one moment thought it right to disparage the faith and experience of ordinary Christians, so no form of charismatic gift – if gift it is – can be permitted to claim a higher, let alone an exclusive, status among the Christian fellowship.

There is indeed a great variety of forms of Christian experience. But one way or another there must be some experiential confirmation of the doctrines of the Creed if the truths about God, the world and humankind expressed in them are to carry conviction and come home to people in their lives as well as in their minds.

THE WILL OF GOD

It is precisely because of what they discern of the nature of God in the story of Christ's self-giving love – to the point of crucifixion – that Christians are called and empowered to live disinterested, other-directed, lives, committed to the values of truth and love. Love of the neighbour in all its ramifications and particularities has long been recognized as the appropriate human response to the God who is love, and who, as we shall see, has revealed his love through incarnation. God's will for his creation is shown, by the way of the cross, to be the fashioning of communities of mutual love, and God's will for individuals is experienced and known as people let the love command take effect in their life together. While it is true that this can be spoken of in general terms – the fruit of the Spirit being listed by St Paul as love, joy, peace, and so on – the ethical implications of Christian belief for each individual are experienced and worked out in a great variety of ways, as the different characters, both of the saints and of ordinary Christian men and women, clearly show. The will of God takes effect in people's lives in very different ways as Christians open up their own lives to the will of God and experience the love of God in doing the will of God.

But the ethical implications of Christian belief cannot possibly be restricted to the formation of Christian character and commitment in individuals, nor even to the growth and maintenance of Christian fellowship and community in the Church. The love of the neighbour enjoined upon Christians is bound to have much wider social and political dimensions, not only in respect of care and practical concern for the disadvantaged and oppressed, but also with a view to the restructuring of social and political life more justly and fairly for all God's creatures. More will be said about this in chapter seven.

Two further observations may be made at this point. In the first place, it is clear that authentic Christianity can have no truck with policies and acts that manifest the very reverse of love. The worst aspect of Church history and of many people's first-hand experience of Christians is the unloving nature of what they see and of what has been done. But, clearly, it is a direct implication of the revelation of the nature of God as love that Christians should repudiate all forms of exclusiveness, intolerance, persecution, self-righteousness, aggression or revenge.

In the second place, given the demanding nature of commitment to the value of self-sacrificial love, it is extremely implausible for critics to assume that Christian belief is a matter of wish fulfilment. Admittedly, a person might well hope or wish that the universe were not a hostile, alien or meaningless place; but when the ultimate meaning and purpose of life are discovered to involve disinterested commitment to others and to the God who made us, the accusation of wish fulfilment may well be on the other foot. I have noticed in the enthusiasm of students and the general public alike for the deliverances of well-known atheist philosophers and scientists an evident wish to be free from the responsibilities entailed by submitting to the claims of love.

SUMMARY

Belief in one God, the Father, the Almighty, maker of heaven and earth, is not a bizarre or antiquated belief. Our existence as personal and rational products of cosmic and biological evolution, together with the values of beauty, goodness and truth which we discern in the whole creative process, now, as always, suggest the need to see the world in terms of mind and value as its ultimate origin and goal. This has always been clear to idealist philosophy, east and west, down the ages. Christianity has complemented these universal insights with a story of special divine revelation, first in and through the history of Israel and then, within that context, in and through the life and teaching, and the passion, death and resurrection of Jesus Christ. Experience of this ultimate source both of existence and of meaning, crystallized as it is in the self-revelation of God as love, has enabled countless men and women to live positive, meaningful, other-directed lives, and to work, often at great cost to themselves, for a more loving community and for a more just world.

CHAPTER THREE

Trinitarian Belief

THE STRUCTURE OF THE CREED

Before proceeding to examine the Christian doctrine of creation from the world's side, in respect, that is, of what it means to understand and experience the world and ourselves as *creatures*, I want to pause and reflect on the very special Christian understanding of God as Trinity, as three in one and one in three. This distinguishes Christian monotheism from all other forms of monotheistic faith, which otherwise have much in common. The doctrine of the Trinity is not explicitly affirmed in the Nicene Creed, but it is quite clearly manifested in its structure, in its three main paragraphs on God the Father, God the Son and God the Holy Spirit, even though those paragraphs are very unevenly weighted.

We have already seen how the short first paragraph on God the Father is highly selective in the attributes it singles out as ways of identifying the basic object of Christian belief. Most, if not all, of what it says – and of what I have said in expanding on that brief selection – may be held to be true of God as such, irrespective of any inner differentiation. Moreover, in Christian understanding, Christ and the Spirit are as much involved in creation as is the Father. And the way in which the topic of the fatherhood of God remains ambiguous between what most monotheistic faiths would say and what Christianity says about the internal Father/Son relation in God has already been noted.

Much the longest paragraph, not surprisingly, is the second. Here the story of the incarnation and the redemption of the world is spelled out in some detail. This story, after all, is what led to the birth of Christianity and to its distinctiveness from its parent faith and from other religions. We shall be commenting on all this in chapters five and six.

The third paragraph concerns not only the Holy Spirit but also the Church, baptism, forgiveness, resurrection and the future life. What it says about the Spirit is partly in terms of function – lordship, life-giving power, inspiration of the prophets – all attributes which might just as well be ascribed to God without inner differentiation, and partly in terms of the Spirit's relation to the Father and the Son, in a clause which has caused more trouble and controversy between the Churches than any other.

Clearly, there is much unpacking and explaining to be done. And just as the Creed itself goes beyond Scripture in spelling out and codifying the implications of Scripture, so we shall have to go beyond the Creed in spelling out *its* implications. At the same time we shall have to show that what is said here about the divine Trinity is not alien to the Creed's scriptural basis.

THE SOURCES OF TRINITARIAN BELIEF

What was it that led the Christians to the belief that the one God of whom the Hebrew Scriptures spoke *had* to be perceived as internally differentiated and indeed internally related? We can agree that it was not a question of independent, rational, religious thought about the reality and nature of God. There are such purely rational considerations as we shall see. But they came later. There is no evidence that religious minds were driven to trinitarian belief apart from the events and experiences recorded in the New Testament. It can be urged that the pure ethical monotheism of the Jews already contained hints of inner differentiation in God. What was said by the prophets about God's Spirit and by the wisdom writers about the divine Wisdom verges on distinct 'hypostatization' (treating Spirit and Wisdom, that is, as virtually distinct divine persons); but only in retrospect have Christians found intimations of trinitarian thinking and experience there.

The first and foremost source of trinitarian belief was the growing recognition of the divinity of Christ and the need to make sense of the relation between the one whom Jesus addressed as Father and the one now called the Son of God in a more than human sense.

It is highly unlikely that the man Jesus thought in trinitarian terms. He addressed God as Father in a particularly intimate way and he was clearly conscious of a unique commission and a unique authority. But God was Father to him as to any pious Jew. It was probably only in the light of the resurrection and in view of their experience of Christ as a living Lord and Saviour and as a spiritual presence in their midst and in their hearts that the first Christians came to think of Jesus Christ as God made man for the world's salvation. Much more will have to be said about this in later chapters. But if Jesus Christ was indeed the human face of God, then the prayers of Jesus to the Father and the intimate communion between the incarnate one and his heavenly Father were bound to be thought of as taking place in God and revealing something like a Father/Son relation in God – love given and love received. We see the intimations of this in the Fourth Gospel's insistence on the mutual indwelling of the Father and the Son: 'Do you not believe that I am in the Father, and the Father in me?' (John 14.10). In this way the first Christians began to interpret the love of the Father for the Son and the love of the Son for the Father not simply as God's love for the man Jesus and the man Jesus' love for God, but as a mutual love in God preceding the incarnation. This, then, was the first source of trinitarian belief – a drawing out of the consequences of taking seriously the divinity of Jesus Christ.

By itself, that would suggest a binitarian rather than a trinitarian conception of God. What led the early Church to posit three, rather than just two, 'Persons' in God was reflection on the gift of the Spirit, an equally strong motif in the New Testament, where the Father bestows his Spirit upon the incarnate Son at Jesus' baptism, where it is promised that another 'Counsellor', the Holy Spirit, will be sent in Jesus' name, and where the Spirit descends upon the gathered apostles at Pentecost. All this *could* be interpreted simply in terms of divine inspiration, but the way in which the gift of the

Spirit was experienced by the early Christians in fact suggests a further internal relation in God rather than just an extended God/man relation. This comes to expression most clearly in the eighth chapter of Paul's letter to the Romans where it is claimed 'through our inarticulate groans the Spirit himself is pleading for us' (Romans 8.26). The implication is that when God's Spirit comes into the hearts of Christian men and women, they are caught up into yet another relation in God, namely the Holy Spirit's response to the Father. The Spirit's intercession, like the Son's prayers to the Father, reveals the mutuality and reciprocity of God's inner relatedness, and suggests that in God there are three personal centres or poles, not two. Hence trinitarian, not binitarian, belief.

The sources of trinitarian belief are not the threefold formulae to be found in the New Testament, such as the baptismal formulae or the Grace, but rather what was revealed of God through the coming of the divine Son and the gift of the Holy Spirit. In each case the reality of interpersonal relation in God, love given and love received, in mutual address and response, was recognized. It was no longer possible to think of God on the model of an isolated individual person. This gave a new sense to the affirmation that God *is* love (1 John 4.8).

THE NATURE OF LOVE

In the light of this revelation, further *rational* reflection on the meaning of the love of God becomes possible. For, if we are unable to posit the fullness of love given and love received *in* God, God's love has no object unless and until God creates a world of persons to know and love him for ever and to be the objects of God's love. This makes creation necessary to God and prevents us from articulating a theology of God as perfect and sufficient in himself. Strict monotheism, modelled on a single individual person, thus contains a very basic difficulty. For one can only predicate the excellencies of interpersonal relation, and especially those of love, on God in relation to us, not on God as God is internally, prior to creation and for all eternity.

This point has no bearing on the number of personal centres in God. It simply suggests a general need to posit internal relatedness in the divine, if love is really of God's essence. It can be argued that we still require God's self-revelation through Christ and the Spirit, and the experience of *their* relatedness to the Father, to appreciate that God is triune – no less, no more. On the other hand, it has been suggested that there is good *reason* to posit not two, but three – and no more – personal subjectivities in God. Love certainly requires mutuality of giving and receiving. Necessarily, we move from the model of an isolated individual to that of at least two persons in relation. But the fullness of love is not captured by this two-term relation. Love's excellence requires not only love given and love received, but also love shared with another. This element in what it is to love unselfishly would be lacking in a binitarian view. Hence there is reason to posit at least three centres in God if God *is* love.

There is no need to go further than this. No further excellencies in love are missing from a trinitarian conception of God, although of course love may, gratuitously, extend itself in the creation of yet more personal centres of interrelatedness and love.

MONOTHEISM AND THE TRINITY

The question now arises whether Christianity's understanding of God as the Holy and Blessed Trinity, as Father, Son and Holy Spirit, interrelated in the mutualities and reciprocities of love given, love received and love shared still more, remains a genuinely monotheistic faith. It looks as if we have moved from the model of a single isolated individual to that of a society of three, as in the well-known Rublev icon, depicting three figures seated round a table. Can we avoid the accusation of tritheism – of explicating the doctrine of the Trinity in such a way as to suggest that there are three Gods, not one? This has certainly been the accusation of Jews and Muslims down the ages, and it has been widely feared amongst Christians themselves, especially in the west.

However, in what has been said in the last two sections, there has been no going back on the fundamental monotheistic insight that beneath the finite universe's multiplicity and change there lies a single, infinite, eternal, necessary ground, best conceived of as Spirit and will. It is only in the light of further revelation and further reflection that that absolute and ultimate personal source and goal of all there is comes to be thought of as internally differentiated and internally related in the way spelled out by the doctrine of the Trinity. Tritheism would involve positing three finite, and theoretically separate, 'divine' persons, externally related. Trinitarian belief holds that the one infinite God consists in three Persons, inseparably related to each other – and indeed mutually interpenetrating – within the single divine reality.

It is often said, again by western theologians chiefly, that 'Persons' is misleading as an answer to the question, 'three what?', when speaking of God as three in one. The Latin *persona* was a mask worn by an actor on the stage when representing a particular character. The Persons of the Trinity are three ways of representing God in his three basic aspects or functions. They are not persons in anything like the modern sense. This line of thought, however, will not do at all. The inter-trinitarian relations cannot possibly be explained that way. The western tendency towards 'modalism', towards thinking of the Trinity solely in functional or aspectual terms – as though Father, Son and Holy Spirit were just different ways in which God appears or acts towards creation – is manifest in such an approach. The model for God as he is in himself is still that of the isolated individual. The difficulty of pure monotheism is neither being seen nor being faced. And there is no way of doing justice to the personal relations between the Father and the Son and the Holy Spirit which have to be acknowledged if we are to make sense of the incarnation and its aftermath. 'Person' has to bear much of its modern sense when used, analogically, of God in three Persons, or of three Persons in one God.

In order to appreciate the force of this point we need to consider the basic analogies that have been used in trinitarian theology and to see why the social analogy is to be preferred to the psychological analogy.

THE PSYCHOLOGICAL ANALOGY

Ever since the writings of St Augustine in the fifth century, western Christian theology has tended to explicate the doctrine of the Trinity with the help of the psychological analogy – that is to say, with reference to alleged inner differentiations within a single human psyche; say, between memory, understanding and will. This undoubtedly has some merits. It preserves the unity of God and throws light on the notion of *inner* differentiation. It helps to show that the notion of three in one is not just a nonsense. Even impersonal analogies – St Patrick's clover leaf, for example: three lobes in one leaf – help to do that. The psychological analogy, of course, preserves the personality of God. 'Word' and 'Spirit' can be thought of as inner self-projections of the divine mind. But it will be clear that the psychological analogy does not begin to represent the interpersonal relations of love given, love received and love shared still more, that constitute the heart of trinitarian belief. It still pictures God on the model of an isolated individual. Even that great western theologian, St Thomas Aquinas, found himself driven to complement the psychological analogy with the social analogy. In answer to the objection that God is not alone because he always has the company of angels and the blessed, Thomas replies that, even so, God would be alone or solitary if there were not several divine Persons. 'For the company of something of a quite different nature does not end solitude, and so we say that a man is alone in the garden although there are in it many plants and animals' (*Summa Theologiae* 1a.31.3 ad 1).

THE SOCIAL ANALOGY

The social analogy pictures God as a society of three individuals, as in the Rublev icon. Only so can justice be done to the fact of personal relation in God and to the priority of communion and love in God, not just between God and creatures. This must mean that there are, within the one God, distinct centres of consciousness and will, between which relations of reciprocity, co-operation and love obtain. Of course the use of the phrase 'three individuals' is dangerous and can mislead.

The three Persons are not separate, externally related sub-
stances, as three finite, embodied, humans are. The one God,
rather, consists in the three, inseparable and mutually interrelated spiritual subjectivities that we call Father, Son and
Holy Spirit. In ultimate reality, communion is basic.

The insistence that the trinitarian relations are internal to
the one God is sometimes countered by the complaint that
such a model of God is not a model of genuine love. For God
is not being thought of as loving someone other than himself,
but rather as loving himself in other modes. But this criticism only reveals the dominance of the psychological analogy.
It betrays the continuing influence of the idea of a single
isolated psyche as basic.

The argument should really go the other way. Just because,
for Christian trinitarian theology, communion is basic, there
must be something provisional and inadequate about the
externality involved in finite, embodied, human interpersonal
relations. If man is made in the image of God, it is not the
human individual, but human persons in relation, who constitute that image. And maybe it is only our bodily individuality
that keeps us separate. If interpersonal relation is of the
essence of our being, then perhaps we may look for an eventual transcendence of our own external interrelatedness, as
mystics – and lovers – have often glimpsed. So the social
analogy also has its limitations.

DEPENDENCE RELATIONS IN GOD?

It has to be admitted that social trinitarianism – the recognition of the basicality of communion in God – was hard to
achieve and has been hard to sustain. It has always been more
strongly rooted and affirmed in eastern than in western
Christianity. And even there – and certainly in the creeds of
the universal Church – there has been a tendency to give the
priority to God the Father and to see God the Son and God
the Holy Spirit as somehow dependent on or originating
from the Father as the very fount of deity. But there is good
reason to be suspicious of this tendency. The whole burden
of the present chapter has been to show that communion is

basic, that God *is* love, that God *is* a Trinity of Persons, eternally interrelated. If this is so, we shall not be too happy even with the venerable language of 'processions' to describe the relations between the 'second' and 'third' Persons of the Trinity and the 'first'. Certainly, as we shall see, the *incarnate* Son depends on his heavenly Father as the one who 'sent' him into the world; but that relation does not necessarily imply an eternal *dependence* relation in God. Of course, 'procession' does not inevitably imply derivation, and it is the notion that somehow the Son and the Spirit derive from the Father that I am questioning. We can still use the language of 'processions', if we like, to characterize the *eternal* relations of mutuality within the triune God. We shall return to this matter when we consider the second and the third main articles of the Creed.

TRINITARIAN PRAYER AND WORSHIP

Trinitarian belief finds its natural home in the context of Christian prayer and worship. In the first place, Christians find it quite proper to address their prayers sometimes to God the Father, sometimes to God the Son incarnate, Jesus Christ, and sometimes to God the Holy Spirit. Sometimes, indeed, they find themselves addressing their prayers to the Holy and Blessed Trinity. Admittedly it would be a mistake to think that the triune Christian God must always be addressed by worshippers in the plural. Notwithstanding all that has been said about the priority, in a specifically Christian doctrine of God, of the social analogy, there is no doubt that for much of the time Christians will follow the example of their Lord in addressing their prayers and worship to their heavenly Father and will continue to use the singular pronoun, 'he' in referring to their God. This is important, not only for internal Christian self-understanding, but also for inter-faith relations. For Christians do not cut themselves wholly off from other monotheists by their trinitarian faith. It has often been pointed out that Christians, conscious of what they share with Jews and Muslims and other monotheists in world religion, will quite naturally assume that the object of prayer and worship in all these faiths is really God the Father.

But Christians worship God the Father in a somewhat different way from fellow worshippers in other faiths. They do not simply substitute a threefold for a single object of prayer and worship. As we shall see when we consider the work of the Holy Spirit in chapter seven, God comes to us in the Person of the Holy Spirit to take us in our prayer and worship into the very life of God. This is partly a matter of our prayers being taken up into Christ's own perfect offering to the Father, but also, as already pointed out, of the Spirit's indwelling our hearts and pleading for us 'through our inarticulate groans'. From within, it is God himself who moves and energizes our conscious creaturely response of praise and adoration, and in the process takes us into God.

This trinitarian framework within which Christian prayer and worship take place gives a much greater precision and interpersonal quality to the transcendence/immanence polarity which is common to all monotheistic faith.

TRINITARIAN LIFE

Trinitarian faith is not restricted to the special modalities of Christian prayer and worship. It is a further implication of the doctrine of the Trinity that human beings made in the image of God not only mirror in their communal and social life something of the triune divine life, but are also caught up into and energized by the Trinity, both here and in eternity.

In the first place, then, the mutualities of love given, love received, and love shared still more in God, the source and goal of all there is, provide the model for human community and human social life. If communion is indeed basic to all being, human life will find its true fulfilment in the gradual realization of forms of interpersonal relation, mutuality and love. This is the very basis of Christian ethics, which, from the start, must set its face against all individualistic, let alone egoistic, ideals of self-realization. Social trinitarianism, of course, has no monopoly on the idea of love. It is a gross exaggeration to accuse pure, undifferentiated, monotheism of bolstering monarchic, even tyrannical, forms of human social existence. The family and communal ethic of the Jews is a standing refutation of that claim. But there is certainly a stronger imperative towards the realization of co-operative and mutually interdependent forms of human community, where God, the ground of all being, is recognized to *be* love in the fully interpersonal sense of trinitarian faith.

But, second, this emphasis, in Christian ethics, on the social implications of love of the neighbour, modelled on the God who is love, is not simply a matter of imitation. Human community is also a matter of *participation* in the divine life. This is true not only of the Christian Church, which, as we shall see in chapter eight, is called to realize in every place a fellowship of mutuality and love, united to its Lord as Christ's 'body' on earth, and indwelt by the divine Spirit of unity and peace, but it is also true of the wider human community in its many different forms, which, so Christians believe, will find their true fulfilment in the end as facets of the communion of saints, caught up for ever into the divine life and love. To this we shall return in chapter ten.

CONCLUSION

This brief sketch of Christian trinitarian faith will have shown what a difference it makes if we really believe that love is the deepest and most basic reality of all. For the atheist, human love, human creativity and human community may indeed be supremely valuable to him or her, but, ultimately speaking, they are temporary and fragile spin-offs of a wholly impersonal and meaningless system of cosmic energy and evolution. For the theist, the world process is an ultimately meaningful affair. The values of human existence are intended and sustained beyond death into eternity. For the Christian theist, the world is the creation, not only of a mind and heart of love, but of the triune God who is love given, love received and love shared still more. This love grounds our very being, calls forth and sustains fellowship and community here on earth and promises an everlasting society of the redeemed, indwelt by God in the end. It makes a difference if, despite appearances, we can indeed discern those spiritual energies and resources at the heart of things.

CHAPTER FOUR

Creation

THE WORLD AS CREATION

So far, we have been considering Christian belief in God. The Creed identifies God the Father primarily as 'maker of heaven and earth, of all that is, seen and unseen'. In fact, as pointed out already, the Bible and the Christian tradition associate all three Persons of the Trinity with the great act of creation. In Christ, according to the letter to the Colossians, 'everything in heaven and earth was created' (Colossians 1.16). And the Spirit is the Creator Spirit who 'hovered over the surface of the waters' in the primordial act of creation (Genesis 1.2).

But what does it mean to see the whole universe in which we find ourselves as God's creation? It means that the universe – its basic energies, laws and constants, the galaxies and stars, the sun and its planets, the Earth and everything on it – is wholly dependent on God for being in being and for remaining in being. The universe exists not of necessity or by chance. It is not just 'there'. It is completely contingent upon God's creative will. Without God's creative and sustaining act there would be nothing other than the eternal triune God. The whole world is simply posited in being by God. It is not formed out of some pre-existent stuff. It is made 'out of nothing', simply willed into being – all the time – by the Creator.

We do not even have to think that the world had a beginning in time. It may have done – as creation myths, Jewish and other, picture it. It may have always existed in cycles of expansion and contraction, as some cosmologists speculate. Or it may be that time is simply one of the created universe's dimensions, so that it makes no sense to speculate what went on 'before' creation. In whichever case, belief that the world is created is belief that everything depends on God for its existence. That goes for the universe as a whole, and for every single thing that it contains, including every leaf of every tree. Of course we can explain trees and leaves, given matter and the laws of physics, chemistry and biology. But that does not explain there being such matter with such specific inbuilt potentialities. The whole system and its results – the tree and the leaf – exist and are held in existence only by God's gift of being. It is sometimes asked what difference the reality of God makes. The fundamental answer to this question is that it makes all the difference, not *in* the world, but to there being a world at all. Without God, there would be no world. In other words, there is a deep, though not obvious, incoherence in the very idea of a world without God.

Created beings certainly have their God-given powers of action and interaction. We can tell the story of the growth of trees, as we can of our own growth and activities. But all these powers are given and maintained by God's almighty hand. There is no question, for Christian belief, of the world's being created in the beginning and left alone, as the deists supposed. On the contrary, the Creator Spirit not only sustains the universe in being and power, but is immanently present to it at every point and time. How we are to think of God's particular activity within the creation and in relation to God's creatures is a topic which we shall be concerned to elucidate later on.

HEAVEN AND EARTH – ALL THAT IS, SEEN AND UNSEEN

We saw, in chapter two, that 'heaven and earth' may well reflect an outmoded cosmology, envisaging an upper and a lower layer. While it is quite possible that God has created spheres other than our own, we shall shortly see some reason to suppose that the creative process concerns the fashioning of a single, gradually evolving cosmos, out of which the domain of finite spiritual existence is being drawn. On this view the spiritual products of the creative process are destined for transformation and immortalization in the 'new creation' of the future, prefigured in the resurrection of Jesus Christ.

But even if we cease to think of different layers of creation in the beginning, Christians will still want to speak of 'heaven' in the sense of that created sphere beyond death where Jesus and the blessed dead already exist in the resurrected state into which we all and the whole of God's creation will eventually be translated. More will be said about this in chapter ten.

The phrase 'heaven and earth' may therefore be detached from an outmoded cosmology, where it referred to the sun, moon and stars above and the planet Earth below, and reinterpreted to mean the whole of God's creation, past, present and future – the whole expanding universe, including our galaxy and planetary system, and also the whole resurrection world, into which all finite persons, fashioned here 'below', will in the end be raised for all eternity. Christianity, as we shall see, is essentially an 'eschatological' faith, committed to the belief that God's creative plan has an eternal destiny.

The phrase 'all that is, seen and unseen', therefore, as already pointed out, refers both to the visible and invisible aspects of the present phase of the creative process and to the eternal future of creation, as yet wholly unseen and only looked for in faith and hope. There are indeed many unseen aspects of the physical universe in its present state. Science itself has long since given the lie to the view that only what is evident to our senses qualifies as real. Theoretically, unobservable entities are part of the staple diet of cosmology and elementary particle physics. But we are more interested here in the mental and spiritual aspects of our present existence: the worlds of thought and felt experience, the moral law within, the dimensions of religious spirituality through which people in every human culture achieve or are granted commerce with the eternal Spirit underlying all things, and also the products of human thought and creativity: ideas, philosophies and cultures, all of which may at present be inextricably linked to some physical mode of expression but which undoubtedly transcend the written words and the books, the instruments and the canvases, and the stones and bricks and mortar that embody them.

As for the at-present unseen world of the future, the realm
of the blessed dead, the transformed, resurrection, world of
God's ultimate intention, this too is God's creation, wholly
dependent for its eternal reality on the creative will and act
of the triune God.

CREATION IN PROCESS

It will be clear from what has been said already that a great
change has come over Christian thinking about the creation
since pre-modern days when it was still possible to think of
God's creation as a perfect and completed work in the
beginning. Largely as a result of evolutionary theory in the
nineteenth century and 'big bang' cosmology in the twentieth
century, Christians have come to see the creation as a vast
process, out of which the conditions for life and the story of
life emerge – a process still going on, and destined for a
perfected consummation only in the end. What this means
for the traditional doctrine of the fall – the belief that the
world as we know it has lost its original goodness, whether
through the disobedience of humankind or through some
more cosmic catastrophe – will be considered later in this
chapter. The present point is simply that it makes more sense,
in the light of modern knowledge, to view God's whole
creation as a gradual building up from below; the patient
unfolding of nature's God-given potentialities for evolving life
and mind and spirit.

Of course, even on the older view, Christianity contributed
much to the idea of history as a linear process moving
towards a future consummation. Given the conditions of the
fall, there was seen to be a need for progressive revelation,
the gradual fashioning over time of a people and a context
for God's redemptive acts by which the fallen world could be
recovered, transformed and restored, by God's 'new' creation,
to its lost perfection, in the end. But it now seems best to view
this 'salvation history', not as a matter of restoration or recovery, but as part of a much longer process of creativity by
which the energies that make for finite life and society are
first posited in being, then drawn together, through cosmic

and biological evolution, into a world – or worlds – of intelligent and interpersonal life, and only then transfigured and immortalized.

While it makes better sense to think of creation as a gradual temporal process from some primal burst of disorganized energy, up through increasingly ordered levels of chemical, biological, mental and spiritual organization, it does not make sense to think of God as himself part of that process. Even if we do have to ascribe some higher mode of temporality to God in the inner life of the Trinity and in God's interaction with the world which God is making, God's own being and God's own story infinitely transcend the world story. Christian theism cannot abandon its conviction of the absolute distinction between Creator and creation, already stressed in chapters two and three.

THE GOODNESS OF CREATION

The Judaeo-Christian tradition has always affirmed the basic goodness of creation. What God had made was 'very good', according to the Genesis story. Christianity can have no truck with any form of ultimate dualism which sees matter as evil or purports to discern a transcendent source of evil, equally ultimate to God, the source of good. Even where the world's ills are blamed on the devil, the devil remains a creature, a fallen angel, originally good, but corrupted by pride. We shall shortly see reason to question literal belief in the devil, but in any case there is no ultimate dualism of good and evil in such a view.

So, according to Christian theism, the basic matter or energy of creation is good, and the intended products of the creative process – the different forms of animal and human life and society – are in principle good. And certainly the destiny of creation – the perfected consummation of all things in God in the end – is very good. But it is important to realize that the overall evaluation of God's creation as 'very good' relates to the whole process right up to its future consummation. One of the advantages of viewing creation as a process leading to a future goal is that its goodness does not have to be read off entirely from its present state, still less from its beginnings.

For there is no denying that the gradual fashioning of a world of life and all the values it contains – the values of animal species and human interpersonal life, society and culture – is achieved at great cost in suffering and evil for God's sentient creatures during the time of their formation on Earth. This is indeed the gravest threat to the intelligibility and morality of the Christianity of the creeds, and it is high time for us to face up to it fairly and squarely.

THE PROBLEM OF EVIL

The reflective, morally sensitive, Christian is bound to agonize over the question why God permits so much suffering and evil in creation. The most widely given reason for atheism or loss of faith is inability to square the horrors of cruelty, war and natural disaster with belief in an all-powerful, all-loving God. Convinced of the love and wisdom of God revealed in the story of Jesus Christ and experienced in so many life-transforming ways, the Christian will inevitably suppose that there *must* be a morally sufficient reason for God to allow the ills that afflict both animals and humans in the present, formative, phase of the creative process. But what could those reasons possibly be?

I will attempt a brief answer here. But I have to preface this attempt with the admission that no explanation will suffice that does not include reference to a future state of heavenly bliss in which all creatures capable of being made immortal, including all life's victims, will participate through resurrection. But that future hope, however sure, does not explain why things are so ambiguous and often so horrific now. The perfected end-state may justify creation at such a cost; but why does it have to be at such a cost?

The most plausible answer to this question takes the form of arguing that there are certain necessary conditions – logically necessary conditions, that is (in other words, it is incoherent to suppose that they could have been avoided) – for the formation of finite, creaturely, persons, intended to

live creatively in love and knowledge of one another and their
Maker. The most obvious of these conditions is freedom.
Persons cannot be pre-programmed to come out well. Their
decisions must be their own. The risk of the abuse of creaturely freedom is part and parcel of finite personhood, at least
under the conditions of its formation. Eventually, in heaven,
finite creaturely persons will be taken beyond the conditions
that make for temptation and abuse into an environment
where indeed all will be well and all will act and interact without the risk of going astray. But such a perfected state cannot
be created directly, skipping the risky process of formation
and growth. Why not?

That is the key question, on which an answer to the problem of evil pivots. Why *must* God's finite, creaturely, persons
be fashioned gradually from below, under conditions that
make for so much agony and wickedness as well as for so
much creativity and good? In the first place, it seems that
some such law-governed, yet open-structured, world is necessary, as a kind of relatively independent base for the finite
person to secure and develop his or her own identity. The
universe functions as a kind of screen between Creator and
creature, enabling creatures to be themselves, in an environment productive of all the values of finite embodied life.
Second, the Earth provides the means for self-reproduction.
New persons come into being through procreation at the
creaturely level. This is an important aspect of their indirect
formation, again enabling them to be autonomous, self-
directing beings. Third, a regular, law-governed environment
is essential to their learning and growth as finite persons. The
environment has to be predictable and reliable if character
and society and culture – all vital human values – are to be
achieved. On this view, our bodily nature is essential, at least
to our formation, whatever our ultimate destiny may be. Once
that is acknowledged, we can appreciate the necessity of the
pain mechanisms to the preservation of the life of organisms.
We can appreciate that it is the very same, law-governed,
structures that are responsible both for the goods and values
of human existence and for the things that *can* go terribly
wrong. There is a sense in which you cannot have one without
the other.

Our rootedness in nature, and our gradually being drawn out of nature into spirit, though necessary to our formation, are not only responsible for the many kinds of accident and deprivation that afflict sentient beings, but also explain the fact that such creatures in the making are liable to temptation. Our emerging freedom and responsibility, essential as they are to personal existence, personal relation and the society of persons, are constantly pulled backwards by egoism and egoistic desires, inseparable from our natural origin. To transcend this origin, and achieve the spiritual values of altruism and love, is our true nature in the sense of what we were made for. But it is not easy or automatic for creatures rooted in the Earth to achieve such a goal.

It may help us to see something of the necessities involved in such a gradual, indirect, process of formation from below, if we consider the impossibility of just positing a fully formed human character in being, without any processes of growth and formation. The philosopher's gambit of imagining that the world might have been created only five minutes ago, with all the apparent traces of a long past, including apparent memories, built in, is really quite nonsensical. We simply would not be the free persons and characters that we are without the actual process of formation and actual history of interpersonal relations that have made us what we are.

Given the necessary condition of our formation, it will not be surprising to find God respecting the structures of creation and acting within, not against, the framework he has made. It is not nearly so easy as we are tempted naively to suppose for God to intervene and cushion us from the effects of wickedness, accident and natural disaster. He can indeed bring good out of evil in undreamed-of ways, as we shall see, but he cannot be expected to contradict his creation by overriding our free will or by tinkering with the environment on which we rely and have to rely for all our moral, interpersonal and cultural projects.

THE OPENNESS OF THE WORLD

It will be apparent that the picture of God's creation that I have been outlining is of a necessarily structured, yet flexible and open, world. I have been stressing the necessities of structure in responding to the undeniably horrific problem of evil that so afflicts the religious, as well as the non-religious, mind. But the whole point of that response was to see the structure as necessary for all the *goods* of creation: for embodied, sentient, life, for the growth of personhood and character, for the development of social and cultural forms of community life. But the structures are not deterministic ones. They enable the emergence of free creatures, themselves innovative and creative in all sorts of theoretically unpredictable ways. The greatness of the drama of creation lies precisely in the fact that it is not all a wholly foreordained process. Rather, God's world is open to the future; and human beings are invited to make and remake the human world in and through their own free acts and relations, all of them under the influence of divine revelation, inspiration, vocation and grace, and not of a uniquely, all-encompassing, predestinating, will.

On this view, the triune God, though never absent from or surprised by what God's creatures do, does not know precisely what form creation's future will take or what men and women will actually do or make. Clearly the divine Creator knows all past and present facts and the range of possibilities open to creatures. God knows what he will do in relation to whatever creatures do, and, most importantly, God knows that, out of his providential and gracious interaction with his creatures, his ultimate purposes in the redemption of the world and the consummation of all things will be achieved. But the precise route through the creative process to that end cannot be known in advance.

Such a view of creation is in any case more consonant with the idea of God's maximal greatness. For surely, it is greater to bring about and relate to such an open-futured creation than to fore-ordain the whole story. And it has to be said that if everything is fore-ordained, the problem of evil indeed becomes insoluble. Mercifully, the Creed makes no mention of belief in predestination, an understandable but in the end unworthy Christian aberration.

Prophecy, on the view developed here, is not exact foretelling of a known, because fixed, future. It is, rather, a matter of inspired discernment of the signs of the times, of what lies deep in the human heart, and of what is likely to happen if people and nations persist in their perversity. The prophet should be delighted if things do *not* turn out as he or she predicts, if, in response to the prophecy, people heed the warning, repent and mend their ways.

OTHER WORLDS

The question now arises whether the universe which we inhabit and whose properties and regularities we have seen to be necessary for the formation of God's human creatures is the only 'vale of soul-making' that the triune God is creating or has created. We have already acknowledged that creation contains spheres beyond the visible and the here and now of on-going history. There is the realm of the blessed dead in which the saints of God already dwell. But they were formed on Earth in conditions which, I suggested, were indispensable. But are there other than human spheres of finite personal life, perhaps interacting with our world, perhaps not? The Judaeo-Christian tradition has popularly been taken to affirm the existence of just such higher realms in speaking of the angels – incorporeal spirits, living in God's immediate presence, unencumbered by mortality, not set – and that must mean not needing to be set – at a distance from God and built up from below in and through a whole evolving universe. It is true that the tradition spoke of a catastrophic pre-cosmic fall of the great archangel, Lucifer, who became the devil, and dragged down with him a host of fellow spirits, tempting and seducing humankind into its own disobedience and alienation. But originally they were all created good as members of the angelic host.

There is at least a case for *not* taking this talk of angels and devils literally. Such belief is certainly not part of the Creed and cannot be held to belong to the essence of Christianity. It is quite possible for Christians, without forsaking the heart of the Christian matter, to think of angels as symbolic personifications of God's own communications with the human world and of devils as projections of the evil tendencies which afflict us human beings individually and collectively just because of the necessary conditions of our formation.

The main reason for adopting this view is that it makes much more sense to see the whole creative process whereby finite persons are fashioned from below in and through a regularly structured physical universe as necessary not simply for the formation of the values of *human* life, but as necessary for the formation of *any* finite creaturely persons. It is a much more powerful answer to the problem of evil if we can urge that only so can a created sphere of personal and interpersonal life be made. Creation, in other words, is indispensably bound up with cosmic and biological evolution. The cost of such an inevitably arduous creative plan is unavoidable.

There are further reasons for 'demythologizing' the devil. Literal belief in the devil is not really an intelligible belief. For what could possibly tempt a pure spirit, unencumbered with the lures of a physical origin, to fall from grace? Why should such fallen spirits be permitted to wreak havoc in nature or the human world? What is the point of keeping them in being, let alone in active interference with the world, if they have rendered themselves wholly unredeemable? And in any case blaming things on the devil distracts us from facing up to the evil in the human heart and from our own responsibility, at least for moral evil.

It is another question altogether whether this one evolving universe, now seen as *the* creative matrix through which the triune God is fashioning a world of life, has reached the level of finite spirit only here on Earth, or whether the universe, whose basic energies and laws undeniably have it in them to produce intelligent life over cosmic and biological evolution might be expected to have produced other, quite different, instances of such life elsewhere. This is the stuff of science fiction, but many scientists think it probable that the billions of other galaxies do include stars with planetary systems that may well have formed the conditions for life – and eventually intelligent life – to have evolved. On the other hand, there is no hard evidence of this, and it has been suggested that the necessary conditions for the evolution of intelligent life involve so many otherwise improbable coincidences that we need to postulate something in the nature of a guiding hand over and above the chance combinations of matter to account for its emergence here on Earth. In that case, it becomes a theological question whether God has providentially drawn the threads of cosmic and biological evolution together only here or whether he has other worlds of life at other points within this one expanding universe. Our speculations on this question have very little to go on. But, again, it might be thought to make more sense, theologically speaking, to see the creative process as uniquely productive of finite spirit here, especially if, as Christians believe, and as we shall be spelling out in the next chapter, God's intention all along is to unite himself to his creation and his creation to himself by incarnation.

A FALLEN WORLD?

If we abandon the pre-modern idea of a perfected and fin-ished creation in the beginning from which, by disobedience, we fell away, and think instead of a single vast creative process, building up the higher levels of reality from below, until at last the human world emerges from lower levels by gradual evolution, what are we to say about the classical doc-trine of the fall? In what sense is this a fallen world? Well, clearly, the human world as we know it throughout its discov-erable history and in all its social forms today falls very far short of God's ultimate creative intention. So much is this fact bound up with what we have supposed to be the necessary conditions of our formation – not only our freedom but our rootedness in nature too – that 'fallenness' in this sense is virtually inevitable at this stage in the creative process. Once we have abandoned the idea of a perfected creation in the beginning, we are bound to find ourselves eliding creation and fall and seeing the gap between our present largely alienated state and the harmony of the intended end-state of creation as an unavoidable gap, requiring further steps to be taken before it can be closed and the alienation overcome. The classical Christian doctrine of the fall and the scriptural stories depicting it may then be taken all as picture language, portraying the human condition as it now is and its evident need for transformation. Of course, the way things are now is not simply the result of our gradual formation 'from below'. As pointed out in an earlier section of this chapter, the state of alienation in which we find ourselves is largely due to our abuse of our God-given freedom.

Again, if the law-governed, physical universe is responsible, not only for our emergence and formation, but also for most of the ills that afflict us on Earth, this too is part and parcel of the world in its 'fallen' state. It too falls short of God's ultimate intention, and is destined for transformation into, or replacement by, God's new creation, the resurrection world, where the arduous conditions of our formation are dispensed with, having played their necessary role.

SCIENCE AND RELIGION

I may insert, at this stage of my treatment of the world as creation, a word about the relation between a scientific view of the world and a religious view of the world.

It is too simple just to say that science investigates and theorizes about *how* the world, with its given properties and powers, actually works and evolves and enables its various products to interact causally and innovatively at every level, while religion ponders and reveals the ultimate *whys* and *wherefores* of the whole process, disclosing its deepest meaning and its destiny. Admittedly, there is nothing wrong with contrasting the respective spheres of science and religion like this; for, certainly, science cannot possibly account for why the universe exists at all and why it contains the fundamental energies and laws that it does contain. Equally, religion has no business to be interfering with scientific study of the world in which we find ourselves, and of ourselves as part of that evolving world – always excepting the ethical constraints within which, as mentioned in chapter one, the scientific enterprise must operate. But this very exception, which concerns not only the bearing of religion on science, but also the bearing of morality on science, shows up at once the inadequacy of any attempt to keep the domains of science and religion apart as at most complementary perspectives on a given world. And indeed our reflections on creation and evolution and on the problem of evil have already made clear how differently the Christianity of the creeds has to be understood in the light of modern science.

The two perspectives interact and affect each other both ways, of course. Modern science has greatly influenced the way in which contemporary doctrines of creation and fall are reformulated. An evolutionary perspective, in which creation is seen as a developing process from impersonal beginnings right through to the emergence of life and personality, is virtually forced upon the Christian mind by the discoveries of science. The explanation of evil is in fact greatly helped by the discovery of the necessary role of organized matter in the evolution and sustenance of all forms of life. It is practically impossible to see the energies and laws of the physical universe as somehow other than what God intended and intends in providing the conditions for the formation of finite personal life. The doctrine of the fall simply has to be 'demythologized' in the light of modern science.

Christian anthropology – Christian understanding, that is, of the nature of humankind – is also greatly affected by the discoveries and applications of modern science. This occurs, most obviously, at the level of medical knowledge, where illnesses previously attributed to demonic possession are now understood as the result of physical, psychological and sometimes sociological malfunctioning. But, much more widely, both the limitations and possibilities of human existence, at the individual, interpersonal, and social and cultural levels are greatly illuminated and enhanced by the applications of the natural and human sciences.

But, equally, religious and theological insights greatly affect not only the way we do science – the necessary ethical constraints have already been mentioned – but also our overall understanding and evaluation of the results of scientific discovery. The need to postulate a 'guiding hand' throughout the evolutionary process has been referred to, as have the theological reasons for doubting the existence of extra-terrestrial intelligent life. But, more importantly, the realization that humankind is being drawn out of nature into spirit, and that the ultimate destiny of evolution's highest products is resurrection, is bound to react back on our sense of the scope of science, and reinforce our doubts about its ability to do full justice to the mind, let alone the spirit. While religion has much to learn from science, and is bound to revise its understanding in the light of science, science itself has much to learn from religion about its limitations and its inability to give an account of all aspects of the created world.

THE NEED FOR REDEMPTION

I return, therefore, to Christian theology and to what it has to say about the human situation and its needs. I have acknowledged that our state, individual and communal, falls very far short of the ideal and of God's ultimate creative intention. Moreover, it is clear that the creative process in which we find ourselves, even with providential guidance and the assistance of divine grace, is not, under present conditions, going to bring about the realization of that perfected consummation in which, in the end, all things will be gathered up in God and God will be all in all. Certainly, the structures of creation, although they have it in them to evolve a world of life, spirit, culture, community and love, do not, of themselves, have the power to overcome the alienation and egoism, to say nothing of the disasters, that afflict humankind. Providence may bring good out of evil, and grace may inspire saintly lives and transfigure human communities, but every generation in a sense begins again and all life's victims cry out for something more. Even in an evolutionary perspective on the process of creation, Christianity remains a religion of redemption, bearing witness to God's acts of new creation, culminating in resurrection. As we shall see, the Creed goes on to speak of these things. For the moment, we simply recognize the incompleteness of the creative process at this formative stage, necessary though that stage may be.

GOD'S ACTION IN THE WORLD

All this means that we have to distinguish between the way God acts in the world now, during this formative stage of the creative process, and the way God acts to transform the world from its present conditions to those of eternity. The two are, of course, not unconnected. The former is a necessary preparation for the latter, and the latter – God's acts of resurrection and new creation – are anticipated in history with the story of Jesus and react back into history with a recreative power not hitherto available. But the fact remains that there are different things to be said about the way God acts in history from what is to be said about the ultimate transformation from history to eternity. In the present chapter, we are concerned only with God's acts in history.

The stress that I have placed on the structures of creation and their necessary role in this present formative stage is bound to lead to reservations on the subject of miracle, at least if by 'miracle' we mean a direct intervention by God that breaks the course of nature. Certainly nature is not a rigid deterministic structure. There is plenty of scope within its flexible openness for God to act freely as there is for us to act freely. But it seems that God, for good reasons already touched on in our treatment of the problem of evil, respects the structures of creation and acts within rather than against them. There may be a few exceptions to this. We shall consider some traditional examples in the next chapter. But, for the most part, it seems best to think of God's action in history as providential rather than miraculous. Consequently, we need to reinterpret most, if not all, the biblical and traditional miracle stories as picture language expressing what in fact were providential acts of God. Of course, if by 'miracle' we mean something novel and creative that excites wonder and religious awe, then there are indeed innumerable 'miracles' in the history of religions.

What, then, do we mean by God's 'providential' activity in nature and in history? We mean the way in which the divine Spirit, pervading and indwelling the whole created order, draws the threads of evolution, history, and all human lives and communities, into closer conformity with God's ultimate purposes for creation. Without forcing or faking the story, God works in and through the forces of nature and the free acts of men and women, to further his designs of creativity and love. In the human world, this often takes the form of inspiration – inspiration of artistic and cultural innovation as well as of religious and prophetic insight. Often it involves the bringing of good out of evil in quite unexpected ways; for God cannot override human freedom or the processes of nature if, as we have seen, they play a necessary role in his whole creative plan.

A key example of God's providential shaping of a particular sequence of events is the story of the establishment and development of Israel's identity and faith that we find in the Hebrew Bible. Christians call this the Old Testament and see its narrative as depicting God's special vocation and formation of a chosen people, inspired to fashion the conditions of faith and the knowledge of God into which, in the Person of his Son, God himself might come amongst his human creatures as one of us, in order to draw us into the divine life for ever.

These matters will be explored in subsequent chapters as I turn to the second main article of the Creed and try to spell out what is most special about Christianity. We shall see how a new phase in God's providential activity is made possible by the incarnation and by Christ's cross and resurrection. For the first time, a foretaste of the *new* creation is given to the world. Christians now experience God's providential activity as grace; and the Church of Christ, in the power of the Spirit, anticipates, albeit fragmentarily, something of that ultimate transformation which is to be the destiny of all creation.

THE FUTURE OF CREATION

All this means, of course, that my account of creation is inevitably incomplete. The ultimate future of creation is a distant goal to which we can only look forward in hope. But in the next five chapters I shall be exploring the way in which God's redemptive and transforming work refashions God's personal creatures into characters and communities that anticipate God's kingdom in the end. The ultimate future lies beyond death and resurrection, but the power of that future is active now, preparing the way. Moreover, the transformation of the old creation into the new, while it certainly involves God's own initiatives in reconciliation, sanctification and ultimately resurrection, is not an automatic process, occurring willy-nilly. At each stage, the love that makes all things new invites our co-operation, inspiring and demanding ethical response in our personal lives, in our Christian fellowship, and in the wider world of human social, national and international life. That is why we shall have to consider the ethical implications of all the doctrines of the Creed, even those concerned with the ultimate future of creation.

CHAPTER FIVE

Incarnation – Jesus Christ

JESUS CHRIST

Christianity and the other monotheistic faiths have much in common: belief in a creator God, spirituality, worship, ethical commitment, to name but a few; but Christianity differs from all other religions most obviously in the centrality it accords to Jesus Christ. This man, Jesus, was undoubtedly the founder of Christianity.

On the other hand, Christianity branched out from an already existing religion – Judaism. Jesus was a Jew, brought up in the faith of Israel. He did not invent the specific form of ethical monotheism which provided him with his own religious perspective. From a Jewish point of view he can be seen as a rabbi, a teacher or a prophet, sharpening and deepening an already existing faith. The Lord's Prayer, which he taught his disciples to use, is an eminently Jewish prayer for the realization of God's kingdom on earth.

Jesus came from Nazareth in Galilee, and grew up in a carpenter's shop. He was drawn, it seems, into a powerful ascetical religious movement, led by a certain John, called the Baptist, but soon launched out on his own, teaching about God and his demands with great power and attraction. He performed acts of healing and other remarkable deeds that were soon recounted as miracle stories. He gathered a group of followers around himself, who were themselves sent out to preach and win others to the Jesus movement.

The Nicene Creed tells us nothing about all this. It assumes that Christians know it from the Gospels and from their participation in the life of the Church. Certainly, the Creed anchors the figure of Jesus in history. It mentions his birth, his mother's name, his suffering under the Roman procurator, Pontius Pilate, his crucifixion and his burial. But its main concern is the full theological significance of his person and work, which the Christians had come to see in this first-century Palestinian Jew.

To reconstruct the purely human, historical, figure of Jesus of Nazareth, we have to do a lot of careful, critical, work. We have to press back behind not only the Christian creeds but also the New Testament itself. For the New Testament too is a heavily theological work, the more than merely human significance of Jesus having been appreciated long before the creeds were formulated. The whole story of Jesus, including his teaching and his deeds, is handed down in the New Testament already coloured by the conviction that he was more than a prophet – that he was the Lord, the Christ, the Son of God, the Word made flesh.

My primary task, in this chapter, is to spell out the full religious significance of Jesus as the early Christians, in the light of their experience and reflections, came to perceive it and to formulate it in the creeds. But, although it took four centuries of debate to hammer out the Nicene Creed as we know it and use it today, the roots of this considered confession of faith go right back, not only to the New Testament, but to the events, historical and more than historical, to which the New Testament bears witness. And among those events were certainly the actual character and words and deeds of the man Jesus himself. He acted and spoke, it seems, with an authority transcending that of a mere rabbi or prophet, opening people's eyes, pronouncing the forgiveness of their sins, declaring the arrival or at least the inauguration of God's reign, and identifying people's response to him with response to God himself.

For reasons we shall see, the Creed goes way beyond this hesitant, initial recognition, even in the first clause of its central, second, paragraph: 'We believe in one Lord, Jesus Christ'. Later in this chapter we shall explain what is meant by the uniqueness and the lordship of Christ. Here, in this first section of my commentary, I want to focus on the word 'Christ', and ask what this means. It has come to function almost like a surname. The founder of Christianity goes by the name of Jesus Christ. His given name was indeed Jesus, a name which in its various forms, 'Joshua', 'Jeshua', 'Jesus', itself has a meaning: 'Jehovah saves'. But the word 'Christ' is first and foremost a title rather than a name. It means 'the anointed one', and was used to refer to the Jewish 'Messiah'. It was a feature of Judaism from the time of the Exile to hope and look for a future saviour figure, usually a king of David's line – though sometimes a prophet – who would free Israel and restore her prosperity and peace. In these senses, the expected Messiah was a purely human instrument of God's purposes of restoration. In some later books of the Hebrew Bible, and certainly by the time of Jesus, these ideas had tended to become confused with more extravagant, 'apocalyptic', notions of a heavenly figure descending from the sky to save God's people. Even so, the 'messianic' movements contemporary with Jesus were more inclined to focus on an actual religious or political leader, sometimes forming an exclusive, quasi-monastic movement out in the desert, sometimes, more dangerously, precipitating movements hopeful of revolt against the Roman occupation.

Out of these very varied but potent expectations, Jesus – or more probably the early Christians, in the light of Jesus' short career and tragic fate but also of his resurrection – fashioned a new conception of God's agent of salvation. In particular, the idea of a messianic 'king' was merged with that of the 'suffering servant' of Isaiah 53, and the religiously powerful conception of a suffering Messiah, redemptively effective precisely through his suffering and death, became the interpretative key in the minds of the early Christians for understanding the significance of Jesus. For, one way or another, it was Jesus of Nazareth whom the Christians identified and accepted as the long-expected 'anointed one' – God's instrument of restoration. But there is no denying that the notion of what 'Messiah', 'Christ', really meant suffered a sea-change.

It may be that it was the resurrection of Jesus from the dead, which I shall endeavour to explain in a later section of this chapter, that confirmed, in the eyes of the first Christians, that Jesus was indeed the longed-for Christ. It was, in all probability, the resurrection too – and the experience of the risen Christ as alive and active through the Spirit in their midst – that opened their eyes to the divinity of Christ. For what undoubtedly distinguishes the Christian understanding of Jesus as the Christ is conviction of his more-than-human nature – not only that he had come into the world from the side of God, but that he was, in a sense now to be explained, God incarnate.

It might be thought that the first-century Jewish messianic hope is a matter of interest only to the Jews, most of whom have, in any case, rejected the Christians' claim that Jesus was the Christ, or to historians of ancient culture. And of course it is perfectly true that the Christian creeds, like the majority of gentile Christians down the ages, are much more concerned with the divinity of Jesus Christ than with his messiahship. That is why my own concern in the bulk of this book is with the meaning and significance of the incarnation. All the same, the title 'Christ' was soon appended, permanently, to the name of Jesus, and the fact that Christianity and Christians bear the name they do is lasting testimony to the fact that the Christian religion is rooted in the faith and expectations of Israel. As we shall see when we turn again to the subject of the humanity of Christ, this fact – that Jesus was a Jew – is central not only to Christian understanding of the providential preparation of the context for the incarnation, but also to Christian understanding of God's providence in human history as a whole. But first we must explore the Creed's apparently extravagant assertions about the divinity of Christ.

THE DIVINITY OF CHRIST

Many world religions owe their principal formation to an outstanding individual – Confucius, Zoroaster, the Buddha, Muhammad, to name but a few. But with the exception of certain major strands of Hinduism, Christianity is alone in believing in the full divinity of its founder, Jesus Christ. Moreover, Christianity is entirely without parallel in holding to the uniqueness of God's personal presence in and as the human individual, Jesus. Very soon, in the light of Christ's resurrection, the early Christians were paying him the worship and devotion due to God alone, and finding in him the revelation and the saving act of God in person. It was not through a representative other than himself that God had now made his nature and will known to humankind. God himself in person had crossed the divide between infinite and finite, and by taking human nature upon himself, lived and suffered a genuinely human life and died a genuinely human death.

The divinity of Christ is affirmed without reserve in the Nicene Creed: 'God from God, Light from Light, true God from true God . . . of one Being with the Father'. In order to make sense of this, as we have already seen in chapter three on trinitarian belief, the early Christians used, initially, a metaphor from human family life – the relation between a father and his son – to articulate the internal personal relation in God which the incarnation disclosed. God was, of course, already known as Father and Jesus naturally addressed him as such. But recognition of the divinity of Jesus Christ led the early Christians to speak of him as none other than the only and eternal Son of God. The primary subject of that human life was God the Son; not a creature, but rather the 'eternally begotten of the Father', now himself a creature by incarnation, but eternally the second Person of the Trinity, the divine *Logos* or Word through whom creation itself had taken place – as the Creed puts it: 'through him all things were made'. We have already seen how all three Persons of the Trinity are involved in the creation of the world.

We are bound, I think, to express some reservations about the term 'begotten'. It is, indeed, part of the Father/Son metaphor that was found most suitable for expressing the personal relation in God, revealed by the incarnation. The stark contrast, 'begotten, not made', distances the Creed's Christology from any view which sees Jesus Christ as merely human, merely a creature. There is no doubt that something like a Father/Son relation is being recognized as being true of the eternal God. But none of the eternal 'processions' in the Trinity – as was pointed out in chapter three – is really captured by a term denoting an absolute relationship of dependence in the triune God. Once we saw reason to play down the notion of the second and third Persons in the Trinity as *originating* in the Father, we were bound to prefer a less one-sided way of expressing the relations between the eternal, mutually indwelling, Persons who constitute the one God of the Christians.

Much depends, in Christianity, on the divinity of Christ. Only by entering the human world in person does God make his love most intimately known. Only by bearing the brunt of human wickedness and suffering in person can and does God take full responsibility upon himself for the cost involved in the creation of the human (and animal) world. As we shall see in the next chapter, only by loving us to the end – to Gethsemane and Calvary and beyond – does God make possible the saving transformation of our human condition from alienation to eternal fellowship with one another and with him. And only by taking human nature into himself for ever – and by drawing us humans into permanent relationship with himself in God – is the ultimate destiny of humankind eventually to be achieved.

All this means that Christian affirmation of the divinity of Jesus Christ is not just an extravagant glorification or 'deification' of a remarkable religious leader. On the contrary, the belief that God, in the person of his eternal Son, entered human history as the man Jesus of Nazareth and thereby took humanity and human destiny into himself represents a whole new philosophy of history and a whole new theology of God. Christians believe that, in the providence of God, human history as a whole is pivoted around that all-encompassing self-presentation of God himself in our midst. By the incarnation and its consequences, the triune God is as fully revealed as he will be this side of eternity, and humankind is for ever taken into the trinitarian life and history of God.

THE HUMANITY OF CHRIST

The incarnation is the supreme Christian mystery. God, in the Person of his eternal Son, came down from heaven – crossed, that is, the divide between Creator and creature – and became a human being. All three Persons of the Trinity were involved in this climactic event as well. God the Father sent the Son into the world. God the Holy Spirit brought it about that a particular people and a particular family were indeed host to the eternal Son's incarnate life; and indeed it was the Holy

Spirit who empowered Jesus to be the human vehicle of God's incarnate life. But it was God the Son who was and is the ultimate subject of that life. This makes Jesus utterly unique. There is an astonishing act of self-limitation and self-emptying here. Without, of course, ceasing to be the divine Person he ever is, God the Son lived out the life of an itinerant Palestinian Jewish rabbi, experiencing human life from within, brought up in a Jewish family, inheriting and interiorizing the faith of Israel, and teaching with a unique authority – its source perhaps unknown to him, at least from the human side – the healing love of God and the searching demands of that love.

For his humanity to be real, the eternal Son could not come to us out of the blue. His Jewish human life, including his Jewish human mind and personality, were the long-prepared vehicle and expression of the incarnate life. This is the providential meaning of his location at that particular place and time, when the developing faith of Israel had reached a point where a particular faithful Jewish family could, without implausibility, become the human context of his birth and nurture. This wondrous event, the birth of God incarnate, is portrayed and symbolized in the Christian scriptures in stories and legends whose historicity we do not have to insist on. But, certainly, *what* they symbolize is no legend or myth. It is the supreme truth of Christianity – Emmanuel, God with us, the incarnation.

And what of the virgin birth – more accurately, the virginal conception? The Creed names the mother of Jesus as 'the Virgin Mary', reflecting the story, handed down in the Gospels of Matthew and Luke, that Jesus had no human father. It is significant that other New Testament authors seem unaware of this. The story certainly serves to emphasize the central fact about the incarnation, namely, that this child was indeed from God, was God made a human being. As already explained, it was the Holy Spirit's agency that brought this event to pass. But it is important to realize that God's agency and human agency are not rivals. The truth of the incarnation does not depend on Jesus not having had a human father. It may still be that the virginal conception was given to humankind as a sign of this unique self-presentation

of God in human form. But not necessarily so. The Church
cannot countenance denial of the reality of the incarnation,
but it can be tolerant of a degree of agnosticism about its
actual manner of occurrence. It makes perfect theological
and religious sense to suppose that God incarnate had both a
human mother and father.

In the next chapter I shall explore the stated purpose of
the incarnation – 'for us and for our salvation'. But, while the
saving knowledge of God made possible by the incarnation
depends on the genuine humanity of Christ – 'he . . . became
a human being', as the new translation of the Nicene Creed
now puts it – it does not in any way depend on the fact that
he was a man and not a woman. A real human life must of
course be one or the other, and no doubt the social conditions
of the time made it more appropriate that God incarnate
should be a man. But no theological consequences, least of all
for the Church's ministry in changed conditions, can possibly
be drawn from this.

For the incarnation to be real, the humanity of Jesus had
to be real. As a human being, he shared a first-century Jewish,
Palestinian, perspective. In all probability, he was unaware of
who, ultimately speaking, he really was. As a human being,
he was probably conscious only of a closeness to God, his
heavenly Father, of the powerful and compelling inspiration
of the Spirit, and of an unquestionable authority to speak and
act for God among his fellow Jews. He shared many of the
demonological categories of the day, regarding what we call
epilepsy or schizophrenia as possession. And he shared much
of the apocalyptic framework of first-century Judaism, even
to the extent of expecting the 'end' within the lifetime of his
disciples. And yet he taught about God – God's love and
God's demands – with an authority and novelty that speak to
us across the ages; and the way in which he went to his death
moves us as no other human story does – witness the effect
of Bach's *St Matthew Passion* even in a twentieth-century secular age.

To stress both the divinity and the humanity of Christ is to
insist that in the incarnation something like two consciousnesses are at work. The divine mind of God the Son, in taking
a human nature upon him, presumably knows throughout

the process – which, after all, lasts through resurrection into eternity – what he is doing and what his incarnate, human self is thinking and doing. The human mind of Jesus was, presumably, something like as I sketched it in the previous paragraph, a mind uniquely conscious of the Father's closeness, love and will. But the two consciousnesses, the divine and the human, were not separate. We should not for one moment think in terms of a personal relation between God the Son and the man Jesus. For the human consciousness and the human being of which it was the subject *were* themselves the incarnate form of God the Son's consciousness and life. As one writer has put it, the latter contained the former without being contained by it. There was one-way access between God the Son and Jesus of Nazareth – of a unique kind, since Jesus was and is God the Son incarnate.

CHRIST'S DEATH AND RESURRECTION

The centre of the Gospels and of the Creed is the story of Christ's suffering and death. The supreme paradox of Christianity is the fact that love incarnate was rejected, betrayed and crucified. The full significance of this will be spelled out in the next chapter when we consider the Christian understanding of the salvation brought about by God in Christ. Here I turn to the subsequent clause, 'On the third day he rose again in accordance with the Scriptures'.

The resurrection of Jesus Christ from the dead, celebrated by Christians every year on Easter Day, plays a pivotal role in Christian belief. (It is, indeed, celebrated every Sunday, the first day of the week, which quickly came to replace the Jewish Sabbath; Saturday, the seventh day.) It was the resurrection that transformed the disciples of Jesus from a disillusioned, scattered, little band into the confident nucleus of a new and rapidly expanding movement. It was the resurrection, in all probability, that opened their eyes to the divinity of Christ, evoking the responses of adoration and worship. It was the risen Christ whom they encountered, sacramentally and spiritually, when they met to pray and break the bread together. And it was in the power of the risen Christ that the new Christian communities became, against all expectation, a revolutionary religious movement in the ancient world and ever since.

But what precisely was the resurrection? Clearly the death and burial of Jesus were not the end. We read of his tomb being found empty and of numerous subsequent appearances of Jesus to the disciples. Conviction that he was – and is – alive and an active resource of grace and power is the hallmark of Christianity from the beginning. But the resurrection was not a resuscitation. Jesus was not raised only to die again at a later date. On the contrary he was raised to glory and that means radical transformation from the conditions of this world to those of the new creation, the resurrection world. His risen 'body' was – and is – no longer the mortal, corruptible, physical body of his earthly life, but rather the immortal, incorruptible, spiritual 'body' of the new age.

By the time of Jesus, most Jews, though not all (witness Jesus' dispute with the Sadducees), believed in just such a resurrection in the end for all. Without that aspect of contemporary Jewish faith, the first Christians could not have begun to appreciate what had happened to their crucified Lord. And Christians today share that hope and expectation of a general resurrection in the end (see chapter ten). What was special about Jesus' resurrection was the *manifestation* of his risen, transformed, person here in history, this side of the divide between this world and the world to come.

The risen Christ was clearly no longer part of the space/time structure of this world. He appeared and disappeared, passing through locked doors. We may well believe that a unique sign of that special this-worldly manifestation of the risen Christ was the empty tomb. But it is quite clear that his risen body did not consist in just those flesh and bones that had been laid to rest. Not surprisingly, the stories that accompanied and expressed the resurrection of Jesus Christ from the dead include some legendary accretions. We can hardly suppose that the glorified 'body' of the risen Christ really ate fish. If pressed on what actually happened to the physical, this-worldly, body of Jesus in the event of transformation that we call the resurrection, we may hazard the, of course tentative, speculation that it was annihilated, as perhaps the whole physical cosmos will be in the end, when it has served its purpose in the creative plan of God.

It is God's plan that the Creed has in mind when it says that Christ rose again 'in accordance with the Scriptures'. No doubt prophecies of Christ's death and resurrection have been read back into Old Testament texts in a way that goes beyond their original meaning. But we can take this phrase as referring to the whole providential preparation for the life, death and resurrection of the incarnate Son. To this, so Christians hold, all Scripture bears its witness.

As we shall see in the next chapter, Christian men and women are called and enabled to share Christ's death and resurrection in both a metaphorical and a real sense. We die to sin and rise again to new life in God. The power of the risen Christ and of the new creation is already at work, spiritually and sacramentally, here on earth in us and in the whole Church, gradually conforming the human world to the shape and structure of God's kingdom. Then in the end we shall all, literally, die and all be raised with Christ into the glorified resurrection world of heaven. More will be said about this in the final chapter of this book.

CHRIST'S ASCENSION

The appearances of the risen Christ to the disciples were of strictly limited duration. This special and unique period of visible manifestations may have been necessary in order to launch the Christian Church, but it had to come to an end. Given the discrepancy between the ending of Luke's Gospel as we have it and the stylized account of the ascension after forty days at the beginning of Acts, we can afford to sit lightly to the actual details of the narratives. Either way, the appearances of the risen Christ ceased. The 'place' of the glorified Christ is not here on earth, but in heaven, exalted and sovereign over all, 'at the right hand of the Father'. Of course, the Father does not, literally, possess a right hand. Indeed, God is omnipresent here on earth as well as in heaven. But heaven is the resurrection world, where God is unambiguously known for all eternity. And that is where the risen Christ, in his glorified and exalted state, has gone before.

The localized presence of God incarnate in history, this side of the transition from the old to the new creation, was necessarily a temporary affair. Only by leaving the Earth could the risen Christ take humanity into God for ever and prepare a place for us in the end (John 14.2). And only by withdrawing his incarnate and risen presence could he come again, spiritually and sacramentally, wherever his followers met, all over the globe and throughout history.

THE PAROUSIA

The last clause of the second main paragraph of the Nicene Creed is one of the most difficult to interpret aright. It has been responsible for much illusion and fantasy in Christian history. Mention has already been made of the 'apocalyptic' genre of Hebrew poetry, associated with the Messianic hope and taken over and refashioned by the early Christians. While some of this material was used to express the significance of Christ's 'first' coming – the incarnation – it was also used, perhaps by Jesus himself, certainly by Paul and the author of the Book of Revelation, to portray the hope and expectation of a 'return' of Christ; a 'second coming' of the risen and glorified Christ, either to reign on earth for a thousand years (the 'millennium') before the end of history, or else to bring history to a close with a final day of judgement. The 'Parousia', as this was known (a word which actually means 'presence' rather than 'coming'), was sometimes reinterpreted to mean Christ's coming again in the Spirit or in the sacrament of the Eucharist. But a more universal expectation of Christ's return, in a glorified form visible to all, continued to characterize early Christian 'eschatology' (the doctrine of the 'last things') and was incorporated into the creeds. The so-called 'delay' in the Parousia was already a problem for the Church in New Testament times (see 2 Peter 3.4).

It seems best to interpret all this as picture language, symbolic not of a literal return or even of the risen Christ's coming again spiritually and sacramentally throughout the

historical lifetime of the Church on earth, real and essential
though these 'comings' are, but rather of his universal 'presence' beyond history and beyond death, where all things will
be gathered up in Christ and Christ will indeed be all in all
– his glory being manifest to all, as the whole human family,
redeemed in Christ, is taken into God to enjoy the life of
heaven, where Christ will reign for ever.

It is at least legitimate for Christian men and women, after
nearly two thousand years of Christian history, to 'demythol-
ogize', thus far, the doctrine of the second coming and locate
its real point of reference in the end time, beyond history. As
we shall see in chapter ten, Christians have a genuine hope
and expectation for the ultimate future of creation, in the sure
purposes of God. And the Christian Advent hope of Christ's
'coming' again and again in ways that constantly surprise us
belongs to the heart of authentic Christianity. But Christians
are well advised to face up to the fact that belief in a literal,
final, 'coming again' of the risen and glorified Christ, back
into the on-going structures of history and the old creation,
makes little or no theological or religious sense.

LORD, JUDGE AND KING

I group together here three titles bestowed upon Jesus Christ
at the beginning and end of the second main paragraph of
the Creed.

Christ's lordship follows directly and obviously from his
being God the Son incarnate. ('Lord' was primarily a divine
title throughout the Hebrew Bible.) 'My Lord and my God'
(John 20.28) was the natural response to the risen Christ, as
his divinity was recognized by the first disciples. But the
nature of that lordship, as indeed of the divine sovereignty in
general which it reveals, is to be gauged not by *a priori*
notions of divinity, or by reflection on the history of religions world-wide, but by the way in which that lordship was
exercised by God in Christ himself. When Jesus' teaching won
adherents among the Jewish people of his day, it was not due
to any exercise of naked power: 'He taught with a note of
authority' (Mark 1.22). It was the spiritual power of what he
said that claimed attention and discipleship. His deeds spoke

even louder than his words. On the night before his death, he washed his disciples' feet, and in the farewell discourses he is represented as saying, 'No longer do I call you servants, for a servant does not know what his master is about. I have called you friends, because I have disclosed to you everything that I heard from my Father' (John 15.15). And the whole way of the cross, the agony in the garden, the passion of Christ, and the crucifixion itself reveal God's way of winning our allegiance to be very different indeed from any earthly mode of lordship or authority.

Christ is indeed our judge. But the final reckoning with our Maker, associated in the Parousia doctrine with the universal manifestation of the risen and glorified Christ in the end time beyond death, is very inadequately portrayed in the awesome sculptures and paintings of medieval and Renaissance art, such as that by Michelangelo on the east wall of the Sistine Chapel in Rome. Rather, as St John recognized, we judge ourselves by our reaction to God's love, incarnate in the life and death of Jesus Christ. Christ is judge simply because and in the sense that he is love incarnate, penetrating to the very roots of our being, showing us the truth about ourselves, demonstrating in action God's forgiveness and God's patient ability to transform us and refashion us into the communion of saints.

Similar considerations apply to the ancient symbol of Christ the King. His kingdom, we are told, will have no end. God's kingdom, we note, for whose coming Jesus taught his disciples to pray, turns out to be Christ's kingdom in the end. In the visions of heaven in the book of Revelation, the Lamb is on the throne. But all these images, drawn from now largely outmoded ideas of human monarchy, are qualified and transformed almost beyond recognition in the New Testament and in the Christian tradition. We have already seen how the idea of messiahship was changed when merged with that of the suffering servant, how the idea of lordship was changed when Jesus, their Master and Lord, washed his disciples' feet, and how the idea of judgement was changed when spelled out in terms of self-awareness in the face of God's forgiving love. So now we see the infant king born not in a palace but in a stable; we see the messianic king suspended on a Roman cross; and we appreciate that Christ's kingship is 'not of this world'. Now and always he reigns in our hearts by the power and attraction of self-sacrificial love. The kingdom of God and of Christ *is* the communion of saints, a fellowship rooted and grounded in love. Christ's eternal rule *is* the rule of love.

AN INCARNATIONAL RELIGION

The nature of the divine love, revealed in action by the incarnation, by the life, teaching, example, passion and death of God made a human being, constitutes the basis and the motive-power of Christian ethics in all its various dimensions. 'Love to the loveless shown, that they might lovely be' – as the Passiontide hymn puts it – becomes the pattern of Christian character, Christian action and Christian community. The way of the cross exemplifies and commends total involvement, no holding back, a willingness to go on working, whatever the cost, for the furtherance of God's 'kingdom' of mutual love and creativity. An incarnational religion is at the same time worked out in terms of social and political involvement. The 'social gospel' has rightly been seen to follow from the religion of the incarnation.

The resurrection of Jesus Christ from the dead in no way contradicts the fact that God's way is the way of incarnation culminating in the way of the cross. On the contrary, the resurrection vindicates the fact that this was and is God's ways of acting in the world – and therefore forms the pattern for the all Christian action here on Earth. If Christians are to live by the power of the resurrection, they should remember that that power, God's power, is enacted and made known in weakness. The resurrection may indeed guarantee the ultimate triumph of incarnate love, but it does not change its nature.

THE INCARNATION AND OTHER RELIGIONS

It is worth adding a note about the way in which the incarnation affects our understanding of the other religions in world history and all over the globe today. As I have already pointed out, conviction that God's revelation and God's saving work reached a providential climax in the life and death of God incarnate rules out of court any unqualified pluralism in the theology of religions whereby completely equal status is accorded to all the world's faiths. On the contrary, the incarnation of God in Jesus Christ necessarily becomes the yardstick by which the whole religious and ethical life of humankind is to be judged.

This need not mean a negative assessment of the worth of other religions any more than it need mean a negative assessment of ordinary human goodness wherever it is found. On the contrary, Christians should rejoice at every sign of God's love and grace reflected in the moral and religious life of humankind. We should delight in the fact that the triune God is evidently at work in the whole human world evoking and sustaining spirituality, mystical experience, worship and devotion, as well as compassion, non-violence, self-sacrifice and love. But the definitive key or clue to the meaning and nature of that love is, according to the Christian faith, given by God's own self-presentation in our midst as one of us, in a life lived and a death died that embodied and expressed God's own self-giving love.

CHAPTER SIX

Salvation

FOR US AND FOR OUR SALVATION

The Creed makes it clear that the incarnation took place 'for us and for our salvation'. That is to say, it is the whole story of Christ's coming amongst us as one of us that brings about salvation for humankind. Admittedly, the Creed goes on to repeat that it was 'for our sake' that he was crucified. But it would obviously be to misinterpret the Creed to insist that salvation centres on the death of Christ alone. The crucifixion is an integral part of the story of Jesus Christ. But our salvation is the purpose and the effect of the incarnation in all its aspects.

It is equally clear from the explicit wording of the Creed that the phrase 'for us' is to be taken in the sense of 'for our sake'. It was out of God's unbounded love for humankind that, in the Person of his Son, he 'came down from heaven' and dwelt among us, enacting in person his self-sacrificial love, no matter the cost.

We can go further than this and urge that the salvation of which the Christian religion speaks is brought about not only by the whole sequence of events from Christ's birth to his death, but by the even wider sequence of events of which the Creed goes on to speak, namely, Christ's resurrection and ascension, and the sending of the Holy Spirit, the life-giver. Indeed only with the Parousia, Christ's final, universal, presence, beyond the death and resurrection of us all, will the salvation of humankind be complete.

What do we understand by this word 'salvation'? Clearly, in

this religious context, it has something to do with saving or
rescuing people from a life-threatening condition of alienation
from and enmity with themselves, with each other and with
God. Its goal is health, wholeness, communion, love. Many
religions diagnose the human predicament as dire. We have
already seen how Christianity perceives the world to be 'fallen',
in the sense of falling very far short of God's intention in
creating a theatre of life, creativity, fellowship and love. The
incarnation was undertaken 'for our sake' in order to deliver
humankind from that parlous state and to bring about that
intended wholeness and union.

Some have argued, however, that God would have become
incarnate anyway, even if the human race had never sinned.
So appropriate is this way of making himself known and taking
us into himself for ever, that it would in any case have been
God's way with humankind. This view has much to recommend
it, although what was said in chapter four about creation
'from below' *inevitably* involving a gap between people in the
making and their intended perfection renders this a somewhat academic speculation. As things actually are, the need is
not simply for a greater and more intimate knowledge of
God, but, much more, for deliverance from the bondage of
sin.

Salvation has both personal and corporate dimensions. As
individuals we are fragmented, at odds with ourselves and
with God. We are beset by egoism and hostility to others. We
need personal salvation, transformation into integrated, other-
directed, creative and loving characters. And as communities
we are divided, and oppressed by alien dominations, social
injustice and innumerable other social ills. We need corporate
salvation, transformation into mutually reinforcing communities of support and fellowship and culture, open to all.
Moreover, as citizens of the global village, we and our whole
world need a sense of the human family as such, a fair distribution of the Earth's resources, and mutually supportive
conditions for the betterment of all the Earth's inhabitants.
Obviously, there cannot be a single, world-wide, face-to-face
community. But the economic and political ordering of
human life needs to be transformed and restructured in order

to support, more fairly, the huge variety of forms of life, fellowship and culture that the human world has evolved and will develop in the future.

The religions of the world, despite their pretty dismal record so far, are in the business of fostering and sustaining these transformations. They make available to humankind the resources of the Spirit for the overcoming of evil and the healing of nations, communities and people. In this sense, all the world religions are religions of redemption. None simply blesses the *status quo*, although they differ as to the radical nature of their diagnoses of the human predicament, and as to the nature of the cure that they deem this predicament to require. Most religions have taught that the betterment of the world will only be achieved through the betterment of individuals, and have therefore addressed themselves primarily to the hearts and minds of individual men and women. But more and more, not least in Christianity's case, that emphasis has found itself having to be matched by the making of proposals and the offering of resources for structural transformation; the key religious doctrines being applied directly to the question of how the common life – local, national and international – can best be made more conformable to the Creator's intention for the whole human family and for the whole world. In the remainder of this chapter, I shall try to expound the specifically Christian way of salvation, asking how what God did in Christ is believed to take effect in the transformation, indeed the perfection, of individuals and communities alike.

LOVE, FORGIVENESS, RECONCILIATION AND ATONEMENT

The work of Christ that brings about salvation is spoken of in the New Testament and the Christian tradition in and through a large range of powerful metaphors, drawn from very different areas and institutions of human life. It is spoken of in terms drawn from acquittal in the law-courts, from military victory, from release from slavery, and especially from the sacrificial cult, so central to the faith and practice of ancient Israel. We shall have to say something about the strengths and weaknesses of each of these metaphors. But first, it is better to try to express the significance of Christ's work non-metaphorically in literal, straightforward, language, so far as this is possible.

The story of Jesus Christ not only declares and reveals God's love for the world, it enacts it in person. 'God so loved the world' (John 3.16) that in the Person of his Son he came amongst us in human form, loving and serving his fellow men and women to the point of extreme sacrifice. Thereby he won – and continues to win – the friendship and the love of at least some of them in return. Directed at all God's personal creatures, this incarnate love eventually will win, by persuasion not by force, the response of the whole human family. Those who do respond in faith and love are united to God in Christ and taken, as a body as well as individuals, into the trinitarian life of God.

This involves, in the first place, the divine forgiveness. That God forgives is not a new idea. It is central to the religion of the Hebrew Bible. But forgiveness is pronounced in person by the incarnate Son to the sick and the unloved and to all who are caught up in the alienated state of human existence under present conditions. And the forgiveness that leads to change is shown to be a serious and costly business by the willingness of Christ to tread the way of the cross. As we shall see, God's forgiveness does not *depend* upon the death of Christ. But God's forgiving love is enacted most effectively where God, in the Person of his Son, is seen to take responsibility for the world's suffering by bearing it himself. Where people experience this costly forgiveness and accept that they are thus forgiven and accepted by the living God, they become open to the Spirit and available for transformation into members of the fellowship of the redeemed, destined to be taken into God for ever.

The least metaphorical of the New Testament words for the effects of Christ's work is 'reconciliation'. 'God was in Christ reconciling the world to himself' (2 Corinthians 5.19); as will be clear from the previous chapter, this verse is not to be interpreted in the weak sense of God's acting in and through the merely human Jesus. God was in Christ in the much stronger sense of personal presence in and as the man, Jesus, whose friends were – and are – thereby the friends of

God. For Jesus was – and is – God the Son incarnate. Reconciliation is a deeply personal notion, suggesting the costly
achievement of intercommunion and fellowship after a period
of alienation, incomprehension and hostility. Of course, it
has to be said that the cause of this previous state lay all on
our side, not on God's. God loves and knows and yearns for
his creatures even in their alienated condition. But there cannot be friendship and union with God at the level of interpersonal relation, until that alienation is overcome. And it is
by the incarnation, the way of the cross and the resurrection
that men and women are won over and transformed into
friendship with God and with each other. Of course, reconciliation normally implies an earlier state of friendship,
lost through rejection and alienation, and then recovered or
restored through forgiveness and repentance. This *was* the
old picture, when the story of a perfect creation in the beginning was accepted literally. But if we were right to see the
gap between creatures and their God – the state of alienation
requiring to be overcome – as intrinsic to the fashioning and
forming of God's creatures from below, then the idea of
reconciliation has to lose that note of recovery or restoration.
The communion and friendship achieved by Christ's work are
something new.

To that extent, the notion of atonement – at least in its literal meaning, at-one-ment – is to be preferred even to that of
reconciliation. For, through the coming of Christ and the
Spirit, we are made one with God in a fellowship that lasts
eternally. On the other hand, atonement has so many other
associations, with conditional forgiveness as well as with the
sacrificial cult, that we may well prefer the utterly personal
language of reconciliation, albeit qualified so as to omit the
element of restoration.

At all events, the effect of Christ's saving work is held by
Christians to consist precisely in the overcoming of that fallen
state whereby, as we saw in chapter four, humanity in the
making falls very far short of the Creator's intention. That
state of alienation is overcome by God's own self-sacrificial
love in action, by God's costly forgiveness, and by God's new
creation of the Spirit-filled community of the friends of God.

THE IDEA OF SACRIFICE

We must now try to make some sense of the metaphors used in the New Testament and throughout Christian history to express the significance of what Christ did to rescue humankind from its fallen, alienated state and bring about that communion with God for which we were created. The first cluster of ideas that features strongly in the liturgies and hymnody of Christendom is that associated with the sacrificial cult of ancient Israel. Christ's life and death – particularly his death – have been regarded as a sacrifice for sin. Most memorably expressed in the prayer of consecration in the Anglican Book of Common Prayer – 'who made there (by his one oblation of himself once offered) a full, perfect, and sufficient sacrifice, oblation, and satisfaction for the sins of the whole world . . .' – and elaborated, much more extravagantly, in such words of popular piety as 'washed in the blood of the Lamb . . .', the idea that Christ's death constituted 'satisfaction', whether in the sense of expiation of our guilt or propitiation of a wrathful deity, is deeply ingrained in many Christian minds. These ideas are rooted in the system of priestly sacrifices laid down in the law books of ancient Israel, but, by contrast with the repeated sacrifices enjoined in the old Law, Christ's once-for-all self-offering to the Father has been regarded as the universally effective sacrifice to end all sacrifices, demanding only the offering of our 'bounden duty and service' in return.

As metaphors for the uniquely and universally effective act of God himself in Jesus Christ 'for us and for our salvation', these ideas retain great power. But if pressed literally, they make little or no religious sense. The idea of a blood sacrifice, appeasing the deity or even expiating sin, belongs to relatively primitive religion, already in the process of being transcended in the Hebrew Bible itself: 'For I require loyalty, not sacrifice, acknowledgement of God rather than whole-offerings' (Hosea 6.6); 'God, my sacrifice is a broken spirit; you, God, will not despise a chastened heart' (Psalm 51.17).

This leads us to reflect on the non-metaphorical, genuinely moral, notions that lie behind the idea of sacrifice. I have touched on these already in my initial characterization of the work of Christ. His whole life, and especially his passion and death, manifest God's costly, self-sacrificial love in action. The moral heart of sacrifice is to be found here in this notion of self-sacrifice: 'There is no greater love than this, that someone should lay down his life for his friends' (John 15.13) – or, we may add, for his enemies and those alienated from him, or for the lost and the unloved. Correlatively, the offering to God of a chastened heart – and the offering of our bounden duty and service, itself spelled out in terms of love of God and of neighbour – are profoundly moral notions.

Satisfaction, or atonement in the sacrificial sense, has to be interpreted morally in terms of the self-sacrificial love of God himself, evoking penitence and the response of a changed and healed, other-directed, life. As we shall see, Christianity has much to say about how this transformation is brought about. It is not achieved by our own efforts alone, simply in response to the example of God's costly forgiveness and love enacted in Christ. Rather, we are drawn into, adopted into, Christ's own perfect response of love and obedience to the Father, and we are inspired and energized by the Holy Spirit to become the fellowship and communion of those who are being sanctified (on this see below pp. 113–15 and 139–43).

LEGAL METAPHORS

Another cluster of metaphors that has a long history in Christian preaching and devotion is taken from the law-court. There is a fixed penalty for human sin: death. Justice requires that this penalty be paid. Out of his great love, the supremely just God, in the Person of his Son, pays that penalty himself, suffering death on the cross in our stead. Thereby we are acquitted and set free.

This too is a powerful metaphor for the liberation brought about by God in and through the story of Jesus Christ. But again, pressed literally, it makes no moral sense at all. It drives an intolerable wedge between the justice and the love of God. And, in any case, what moral sense is there in the notion that perfect justice requires, or could be satisfied with, the death of an innocent man?

The moral truths behind these metaphors need even more
digging out than was the case with the idea of sacrifice. In the
first place, death is not really a penalty for sin. Our literal
death is a perfectly natural aspect of our inevitably limited
lifespan here on Earth in this first phase of God's creative
plan. Nothing that God did in Christ removes the certainty
that one day we shall die. Spiritual death – separation and
alienation from God – is indeed bound up with human sin.
But it is the consequence of sin, not its penalty. It is a deeply
moral truth that egoism, aggression, hatred and injustice lead
inexorably to the fragmentation and collapse of human
integrity, both individually and socially, as well as to separation
from God. People get trapped in these predicaments and find
themselves inevitably cut off from the sources of personal,
interpersonal, and communal well-being. What people need,
if things are to be changed and this alienation overcome, is not
the payment of a penalty, but forgiveness, genuine repentance
and real transformation.

Certainly, the truths of our self-inflicted predicament have
to be faced. There can be no easy, casual, forgiving and for-
getting. What enables people to face up to the truth about
themselves is precisely the costly forgiveness both shown and
pronounced by Christ in the course of his whole mission from
his baptism to his death on the cross. The first stage of our
transformation is achieved when we are won over by that great
love and come to realize that we are forgiven and accepted,
notwithstanding our sin. But that is only the first stage. We
are not deemed just by a legal fiction. We have to be *made*
just.

This leads me to insert a word about justification by faith
– the watchword of the Reformation and one of the most
powerful motifs in Christianity. The phrase is shorthand. It
expresses neatly the heart of the Christian gospel that we do
not have to earn salvation by our works. All we need is faith
in what God has done in loving us into fellowship with God
and with each other. Of course it is not faith that brings all
this about. It is actually done by God's own acts of love and
grace and inspiration. And justification – to repeat – is not a
legal fiction. It is a matter of being accepted and forgiven,
prior to our gradual transformation.

RELEASE FROM SLAVERY

An even more powerful set of metaphors bringing out the fact and nature of our salvation comes from the institution of slavery and from the way a slave's freedom could be purchased for a price. This is where the notion of redemption is most at home. To redeem is to purchase someone's freedom. We can appreciate the force of this metaphor in societies where slavery was a time-honoured reality. No wonder the gospel, put in these terms, spoke so powerfully to the enslaved blacks in the American deep south before their civil war.

Moreover, it is a very good metaphor – both for the state of bondage to sin and alienation in which we find ourselves and for the cost to God himself in the passion and death of his incarnate Son through which our release and liberation are, initially, brought about. But, as with the other metaphors, it cannot possibly be taken literally. The idea that we are in the devil's possession, and that the devil is bought off by the cruel death of God's incarnate Son, is morally and religiously grotesque, and in any case makes no sense once literal belief in the devil is abandoned. Here, then, is a clear example of the difference between the moral and religious truth expressed and conveyed by a powerful metaphor and the moral and religious absurdity of pressing such a metaphor literally. When we speak or sing of the price paid by the perfect God–man, Jesus Christ, in his suffering and death on our behalf, we are using this metaphorical language to express the costliness of the divine acceptance and forgiveness. There was no holding back. God in Christ was willing to tread the way of the cross in order to draw us to himself and set us free to enter into union with each other and with God.

CHRIST THE VICTOR

The most readily intelligible metaphor for what Christ achieved through the incarnation and the cross is the metaphor from victory in battle. The enemies are sin and death and these are defeated in the sense that sin is forgiven and known to be forgiven and its effects overcome. Of course, its effects do not suddenly vanish away. The immediate result of Christ's 'victory' is that those who embrace it in faith are united with God in Christ. Their alienation from God is indeed overcome. But of course there are long-term 'mopping-up operations' as our lives and our communities are rebuilt, transformed and refashioned into greater conformity with God's intention. A key aspect of Christ's victory over death is, undoubtedly, the resurrection, rightly celebrated in Easter hymns as the supreme triumph. And indeed the promise of resurrection to eternal life beyond our literal death is the least metaphorical aspect of the idea of Christ the victor. But the power of the resurrection, so Christians hold and discover in their own lives and in the fellowship of the Church, is already effective, as the Spirit of the risen Christ 'returns' to carry out the long-term work of transformation. More will be said about this in the next chapter, where we consider the Person and work of the Holy Spirit more explicitly.

Military metaphors abound in the New Testament and in the Christian tradition for what I have rather crudely dubbed the 'mopping-up operations' consequent upon the whole story of Christ's life and death and resurrection. We are urged to put on the whole armour of God, to take up the sword of the Spirit, and to fight the good fight. All this is quite clearly metaphorical and may indeed have outlasted its usefulness in an age when war has lost its glamour. There are other ways of speaking of the resources of the Spirit and the transformations that are taking place.

But the basic underlying idea of Christ the victor remains a powerful metaphor for the reconciliation achieved by God in Christ. Indeed, as we shall see in a moment, that reconciliation – and thus the effectiveness of what God did in Christ – extends beyond the explicit, conscious, response of those who put their faith in Christ's victory. The spiritual resources that have defeated and continue to defeat the powers of sin and death are operative, in hidden ways, throughout the human world.

As with Christ's messiahship, kingship and lordship, his victory remains paradoxical in that it is certainly not the victory of irresistible force or crude omnipotence. (On this, see pp. 96ff above.) God's strength is made known in weakness, and

Christ's victory is the victory of patient, self-sacrificial, love. Even in the context of the Christian hope of resurrection, we cannot forget that it is the crucified one who was raised from the dead; and there is a sense in which, as an old saying has it, Christ remains on the cross so long as the last sinner remains in hell.

It hardly needs repeating that Christ's victory cannot be thought of, in literal terms, as a victory over the devil. Indeed one of the fruits of Christ's victory is freedom from the temptation to personify the evil in the human heart and in the human world and thus to divert responsibility for the mess we humans have made of things. It is enough and more than enough that, through God's grace in Christ and the Spirit, the alienation of humanity from God is overcome, and the power of sin defeated once and for all.

THE DEATH OF CHRIST

At this point we need to draw together the threads of what has been said about the death of Christ and its place in the story of our salvation. I have been urging that we should not suppose that Christ's death on the cross was literally an expiatory or propitiatory sacrifice, a substitutionary penalty, or a necessary price for our redemption. Rather, these ideas are at best powerful metaphors for the costly self-sacrificial love of God enacted and made known through God's readiness to tread the way of the cross himself in the Person of his Son. The death of Christ does not achieve anything by itself. To repeat, it is not a condition of God's forgiveness and acceptance of his wayward human creatures. What the death of Christ does is, first, to manifest unequivocally the fact and the nature of God's forgiving love; second, to show God's willingness to take responsibility upon himself for the creation of a world so much at risk to suffering and evil; and, third, as the culmination of his life and ministry on Earth, actually to win our free response of gratitude and acceptance that we are accepted, despite the mess the human world is in. To appreciate the moral force of the cross of Jesus Christ, it has to be seen not in isolation but in the whole context of the incarnation. God's love for the world that he is making leads him to express his solidarity with humankind by coming amongst us as one of us. By this incarnation, he puts himself at risk of rejection and, as it happened, crucifixion. But that is how his self-sacrificial love and costly forgiveness begin to become effective. Human hearts are captured by the divine love present and suffering to the point of a cruel death.

Christ's death on the cross was not the end of the story. The resurrection and the ascension of Jesus Christ mean that humanity is permanently taken into God, and, as we are won over, forgiven and accepted, and refashioned by the Spirit of Christ, crucified and risen, we are made members of his 'body' and taken with him into God.

VICARIOUS SUFFERING

Comment has already been made on the idea, still popular in some Christian circles, that Christ took our place in paying the penalty for sin or in offering a substitutionary sacrifice. We are bound to question the moral and religious sense of these notions. Indeed, the notion of substitutionary sacrifice improperly conflates two very different features of the early faith of Israel, namely the idea of expiatory sacrifice and the idea of the scapegoat bearing away people's sins. (After all, the scapegoat was driven away, not killed.) But can we find any deeper, more truly moral, meaning in the idea of vicarious suffering? Certainly, Israel came to find redemptive signifi-cance in the suffering of the martyrs. Most memorably in Isaiah 53, the Suffering Servant, symbolic of Israel herself, is portrayed as rejected and afflicted for the sake of all God's people. Admittedly, this idea is combined there with the notion of substitution, in a way that cannot, morally speaking, be taken over as it stands. But the real moral force of the picture of the Suffering Servant lies in his readiness to endure and to bear affliction on behalf of others. It is not surprising that this text was quickly applied to Christ and seen as foreshad-owing his passion and death. Sadly, it was also responsible for some of the less acceptable connotations of vicarious suffering.

But there *is* a sense in which God, in the Person of his Son, comes into our place, taking the burdens of humanity upon himself, so that we may be drawn into God's 'place', forgiven and transformed. But this exchange is effected not by substitution but by a costly *solidarity* that wins response and opens up the way to the Spirit's indwelling and new creative work, both in the human heart and in the human community.

When it is said that the blood of the martyrs is the seed of the Church, it is not implied that martyrdom has an automatic hidden regenerative effect. Rather, it is the *influence* of the martyrs' self-sacrifice and trust in God that draws people into the Christian community. Similarly, the passion and the death of God's incarnate Son work first by *influence*, breaking resistance simply by moral persuasion. But in Christ's case, it is not only a matter of influence. For, unlike the case of the martyrs, the Spirit of Christ crucified and risen is a living, active, spiritual resource at work transformatively in our lives and in our communities. There is good reason to mistrust what are called 'exemplarist' or merely 'subjective' theories of the atonement, as though the effectiveness of what God did in Christ was nothing but the exertion of moral influence. But the objectivity of the atonement lies not in something automatically brought about by Christ's death, whether through a legal fiction, an exchanged penalty, or a substitutionary sacrifice, but rather in the on-going work of God, by the Spirit, in actually changing people, individually and corporately, into the fellowship of the redeemed. And this, to repeat, is done by their being conformed to Christ, adopted into his risen body, and taken with him into the living God.

I do not want to be too hard on the notion of substitutionary sacrifice. After all, one who sacrifices his life to save another does effect a kind of substitution. But in the case of our reconciliation with God the dynamics of Christ's sacrifice are very different from those of self-sacrifice in war or the self-sacrifice of a fireman, say, achieving a rescue at the cost of his own life. For what makes life – spiritual life, eternal life – possible for us is not Christ's death in our place, but his costly, self-sacrificial love, that wins our repentance and enables our transformation. To repeat, it is God's *solidarity* with sinners through the incarnation and the cross of Christ that overcomes our alienation and draws us into fellowship with him.

JUSTIFICATION AND SANCTIFICATION

Christian reflection on the salvation that Christ brings is bound to swing, like a pendulum, between the subjective and the objective poles. Much of what has been said in this chapter concerns the former – our eyes being opened to the revelation in Christ of God's forgiving love and our initial response of penitence and faith. This was most movingly expressed in a little medieval lyric, memorably set to music by Benjamin Britten in a late work, *Sacred and Profane*. For our purposes, the medieval English has to be modernized:

> When I see on the Cross
> Jesu my lover
> And beside him stand
> Mary and John,
> And his back scourged,
> And his side pierced
> For the love of man,
> Well ought I to weep
> And sins to abandon
> If I know of love,
> If I know of love,
> If I know of love.

But, increasingly, one comes to recognize the more objective side of what God *does* in us, through Christ and the Spirit, to transform us and to refashion us personally and communally. If justification is a matter of being accepted and forgiven, we are bound to press on at once to what the Christian tradition calls sanctification – being made holy – a notion which, again, has both an individual and a social dimension. More will be said about this in the next chapter; for the work of sanctification is traditionally ascribed to God the Holy Spirit. But the Spirit is the Spirit of Christ crucified and risen just as much as he is the Spirit of God the Father at work in the world. We cannot divide the mutually interpenetrating Persons of the Holy Trinity in their work any more than in their nature. It is God who both by revelation and by inspiration transforms

the human character and the human fellowship, changing
and creating us anew in God's image and likeness, as we are
made one with God.

It is tempting to say that faith must come first and that only
where faith is found can God's saving work begin to take
effect. But just as we have come to see that penitence is not a
*pre*condition of forgiveness, so we learn that faith is not a *pre*-
condition of God's salvific work, but rather is the eventual,
hoped-for, product of a transforming process that is going on
all the time. This assertion may seem hard to take; for surely
the Christian gospel is the proclamation of something new –
God's saving act in Christ – that has to be made known to
people and appropriated by them consciously in faith, before
ever salvation can begin to take effect in lives made whole and
free. These saving truths are indeed to be proclaimed; and, as
we shall see, the Christian Church is indeed the self-conscious
and explicit focus of the knowledge and celebration of God's
reconciling and transforming work. But the fact remains that
the truths appropriated in faith and proclaimed in the Gospel
are more all-embracing and more universal in their efficacy
than simply in the hearts and minds and lives of Christians
and in the fellowship and witness and worship of the
Christian Church.

This becomes clear when we think of *what* it is that faith
responds to and is evoked by. The story of Christ's life and
death and resurrection is, after all, the revelation of the *eternal* love of God. The God whose nature – costly, self-giving
forgiveness, grace and love – is revealed in the way of the
cross is at work in the world all the time; and that means prior
to and beyond the sphere of explicit human acknowledgement
of the revelation. The divine Word, who was and is incarnate
in and as Jesus Christ, is 'the true light' who 'gives light to
everyone' (John 1.9). And the Spirit of Christ crucified and
risen, sent into the hearts and midst of the disciples to lead
them into all truth, is the universal Spirit of the living God,
brooding over the whole creation and inspiring humankind
with all manner of forms of spirituality and creativity. Of
course, it matters that the final focusing of God's salvific
work in Christ and the Spirit should be acknowledged and
proclaimed; but that work cannot be restricted to the sphere

of explicit Christian faith, if the God revealed there is indeed revealed to be the God of the whole Earth.

OTHER RELIGIONS AND THE HIDDEN WORK OF GOD

These reflections enable us to think more positively of the history of religions world-wide and indeed of secular human goodness 'outside the Covenant' – to use a classical Judaeo-Christian phrase. They enable us to welcome and co-operate more enthusiastically with men and women of good will who belong to other faith traditions, including that of secular humanism. Christians in the past have tended to disparage other religions as at best merely human attempts to penetrate the world of the spirit, and at worst tissues of illusion, error and malpractice. For much of their history, both Catholics and Protestants have denied the possibility of salvation outside the Church or outside explicit faith in Christ. Catholics have been more willing than Protestants to extend the boundaries of the Church to include those with implicit faith or those whose good will, even sanctity, seems to suggest the hidden work of God; but only since the Second Vatican Council in our own time has the Roman Church accorded positive value to the other great religions of the world as such.

There are two main reasons why we must reject the old exclusive attitudes of Christianity. One stems from the knowledge of God revealed in Christ himself, the other from our increased knowledge of the other faiths themselves and of what they have in them to foster by way of spirituality and value. This includes the many forms of high culture that the religions of the east and the Islamic world have produced, as well as the personal, family and communal values that Christians have no business to condemn.

But the first reason for not disparaging other religions is the most important from the point of view of Christian understanding. I have already insisted in chapter three that the God worshipped in the great monotheistic faiths must, in the end, be thought of as the same ultimate reality as the triune God revealed through Christ and the Spirit, and that it makes no moral or religious sense to suppose that the God of love, whom Christians come to know in Christ, can or will reject and condemn the non-Christian majority of human beings in world history. But the facts stressed in the last section – the fact that the Word incarnate in Jesus Christ *is* the light that enlightens everyone, and the fact that the Spirit of Christ crucified and risen *is* the Spirit of the God of the whole Earth, active in all creativity and inspiration – should help us to see that the energies of God are at work throughout the history of religions, evoking the manifold responses of humankind not only in and through the religions of the world but also through the human conscience in all spheres of ethics and morality.

Of course, there is much error, illusion and malpractice in the history of religions, but that includes Christianity, whose record, in human terms, often belies the Gospel message of peace and goodwill to all. We saw in chapter one how this sad fact constitutes one of the most telling objections to Christian belief. But just as we have to look for the essence of Christianity in what the story of Christ reveals about the nature of God and God's activity, so we have to look for the essence of religion in the positive forms of spiritual, moral and cultural life that this same God has elicited from his human creatures everywhere.

I speak of this as the *hidden* work of God, since I remain convinced that what God reveals of himself by his presence and activity here on Earth in the person of his incarnate Son, Jesus Christ, goes beyond what he reveals through enlightenment and inspiration elsewhere; and I speak of this as the hidden work of *God* rather than, say, of the unknown *Christ* of other religions since, although it *is* the same Word and the same Spirit at work throughout the whole history of religion and ethics, it seems better to reserve the name of Jesus Christ for the unique incarnation in which God's revelation and salvific work culminate.

UNIVERSAL TRANSFORMATION: THE TAKING OF HUMANITY INTO GOD

It has been pointed out more than once already that God's saving work in and as the man Jesus is not simply a matter of self-revelation. The incarnation is not only the climax of God's revelation of his nature and will; it is the climax of humanity's response to God. With the resurrection and ascension of Jesus Christ, humanity is taken into God for ever and all other responses are being taken up and will eventually be perfected through being conformed to Christ and drawn into union and communion with him. Once again, this process takes place at many levels, not simply at that of explicit, conscious response. While it matters that God's saving work in Christ should be made known and accepted and celebrated consciously in Christian lives, in Christian communities and in Christian worship, it is effective at other levels too. Humanity is being drawn into God wherever the Word and the Spirit are active in religious and ethical enlightenment and inspiration, and in the end, as Christian 'eschatology' – the doctrine of the 'last things' – makes clear (see the final chapter of this book), it will be through the risen and ascended Christ that all men and women from every age and every place will be united with the living God. In that final chapter we shall have to ponder the question whether 'all' really means all, and whether Christian universalism – the belief that all God's personal creatures will be saved; that is, forgiven and transformed into members of the 'body' of Christ – is true, or can at least be seriously hoped for. We shall be asking whether the Christian hope is for a time when not only death but also hell will be no more.

THE SALVATION OF THE WORLD

In that chapter we shall also have to give some thought to the question whether God's salvific work in Christ extends beyond the sphere of what I called God's personal creatures; that is, the human world (if we were right to reject both the angelic and the extra-terrestrial as possible spheres of rational, personal, creaturely existence). So far I have presented the essence of Christianity in highly anthropocentric terms. Whatever other values are achieved and celebrated throughout the whole creative process, the ultimate purpose of creation has been envisaged as the drawing out of nature of a spirit-filled community of persons – that is, rational, self-conscious, free subjects of moral agency and of interpersonal relation and love. Humans alone, on this view, are made in the image of God and destined for eternity. For only those capable of entering the world of the spirit can thus be immortalized by the salvific, recreative energies of the living God. Minerals, plants and brute beasts simply do not possess the relevant capacities for genuinely spiritual life and communion.

There are a number of reasons why we may, on further reflection, be led to qualify and modify this stark anthropocentrism. Certainly, it is wrong to conclude that everything else in creation is merely instrumental to the existence and future of the human world. We have urged that creation, through evolution from below, is necessary for the production of relatively independent, free, creaturely persons in relation, if ever they are to acquire character and build communities and cultures for themselves, and if ever they are to be drawn into the world of the spirit without being overwhelmed. But this creative process is immensely fertile in the production of other values on the way. Seas, lakes and mountains, trees, flowers and vegetables, fish, birds and animals, as well as serving the needs of human beings have a value and a beauty in their own right; and they are very properly extolled in the *Benedicite* ('O all ye works of the Lord, bless ye the Lord . . .') and in St Francis' famous prayer ('Praise be to you, my Lord, for Brother Wind . . ., for Sister Water . . ., for Brother Fire . . ., for our Sister Earth, who sustains and governs us, and produces varied fruits with coloured flowers and herbs'). Their use is certainly permitted, but their conservation and celebration are unquestionably a duty for humankind here on Earth.

But even if these fellow creatures are not in themselves immortalizable, lacking, as they do, the spiritual capacities to become God's children and members of Christ's risen 'body', we may nevertheless hazard the speculation that something of their value will be carried over by association with us into the resurrection world. For humans, we are assured, are not to be raised in isolation from an environment and a world. In this sense Christ is the saviour not only of all men and women but also of the world. To put it another way, the human world includes its environment, and thus the whole creation is destined for transformation into the kingdom of heaven. This is pictured, in highly figurative language, as God's holy mountain, where the wolf and the lamb shall feed together, and the lion eat straw like the ox (Isaiah 65.25). We can hardly expect this literally. It is difficult to see how even the lives and characters of domestic animals can be given eternal life except in memory. But the two factors stressed here – conviction that resurrection will involve a resurrection *world*, and conviction that some subhuman creatures may in some way share eternity by association with the interpersonal life of humans – may enable us to resist the view that the values of the non-human world are wholly temporary and inevitably transitory.

PRESENT ETHICAL IMPLICATIONS

These reflections on the wider long-term implications of salvation may have reinforced the age-old suspicion that Christianity is primarily interested in another world, and that its hope of heaven can only divert our attention and our energies away from the pressing needs of men and women here and now, and from the present need to conserve and cherish our fragile, vulnerable, planet. But that would be a superficial view. As pointed out already, the power of the resurrection reacts back on life in the world in every age, and the hope of a perfected future consummation energizes the commitments that make for personal and social transformation here and now.

We are, after all, talking about the spiritual resources that underlie the whole creative process and are made available to us, through enlightenment and inspiration, for the overcoming of evil, alienation and mutual hostility here on Earth. Those who hold that there are no such resources and that human beings are alone in the universe, the chance products of the interactions of mindless energies and forces, may succeed for a while in constructing positive and creative forms of life on Earth; but, on their own reckoning, they are left to their own devices, and have no basis for long-term hope that goodness and love will in the end prevail. Religious conviction, by contrast, and in particular Christian resurrection faith, draws on what are believed to be the energies of God, the Creator, the Revealer and the Reconciler, for the fashioning and sustaining of spirit-filled communities in which individuals are made whole, relationships healed, and creative forms of life and culture enabled to develop.

It is no longer seen as a matter of luck whether the human world gradually becomes more just and more holy. The divine providence, operating admittedly through recurrently wayward human material, is leading human history in a one-way direction that will eventually result in the perfected consummation of heaven. Of course, it is a slow process, if the means are those of self-sacrificial love and grace, not those of limitless power. And each new generation of humans has to be introduced to the claims of the Spirit, and integrated into the processes of transformation. But we do not each time start from scratch. The on-going story of God's salvific activity is there to be appropriated and developed, and the same spiritual energies are there to be drawn on. We have the example of the saints, and of family and social life informed by qualities of mutual support and care – lives and communities that manifest the fruits of the Spirit. And there are discernible signs, despite everything, that the world is becoming more just and more humane. At the very least we are much more aware of the enormity of injustice and inhumanity where these are to be found.

CHAPTER SEVEN

The Holy Spirit

THE HOLY SPIRIT, THE LORD

The third main paragraph of the Creed begins with an affirmation of Christian belief in the Holy Spirit. And, just as the title 'Lord', which in the Hebrew Bible was used unequivocally of God himself, got transferred by the Christians to our one Lord, Jesus Christ, thus marking *his* divinity, so the Holy Spirit is immediately characterized as 'the Lord', thus marking Christian conviction that the Spirit, too, is God. This takes up the saying in 2 Corinthians 3.17: 'Now the Lord . . . is the Spirit'. So the first thing to be affirmed here is the divinity of the Holy Spirit. The Spirit is in no way to be thought of as some *created* energy permeating the world or enlivening the Church.

Actually, Christians today are seldom tempted by the idea of the Spirit as a created energy. We find no difficulty in speaking of God as Spirit and of the Spirit as God active in the world and in the Church. It seems quite natural to Christian believers today to think of God's Spirit creatively and recreatively at work by grace and inspiration. Our difficulty, rather, is to see why Christians hold the Holy Spirit to be a distinctive divine Person in the Holy Trinity, a third centre or subject in God, not to be confused with God the Father and God the Son, albeit intimately related to the Father and the Son and inextricably involved with them in creation, revelation and reconciliation.

I must refer back at this point to what was said, in chapter three, about the divine Trinity and to the rational, revelatory and experiential sources of belief in the Holy Spirit as a distinct Person in God. Rationally, it will be recalled, we need to posit three, not two, personal centres in God if God *is* love; if, that is, the excellencies of love given, love received and love shared still more are to be discerned in God as such, not just in God's relations to creatures. Divine revelation not only discloses God's nature as love through the relation between the Father and the incarnate Son, but also through the way in which the Spirit is both sent out into Christian lives and Christian communities and received back, where humanity, first in and through the Christian Church, is being drawn into the trinitarian life of God. The revelatory and the experiential dimensions are inextricably linked together, since it is in prayer and worship that the distinct divine reality of the Holy Spirit is experienced by believers. In their faltering prayers they find themselves caught up in God's own self-address, as the Spirit within them lifts their praises and their pleading to the Father. And in their worship as a Church they find themselves caught up likewise into the divine Trinity, participating, however haltingly, in the process of mutual intercommunion that constitutes the divine. The Spirit takes up our human liturgy into God's own internal movement of reciprocal return.

In much human religion God is experienced and thought of as 'wholly other' – the object of numinous awe over against the worshipper or the devotee, claiming people's obedience and allegiance in a supreme 'I–Thou' encounter, typified by Isaiah's vision in the Temple (Isaiah 6.1–5). The Judaeo-Christian tradition speaks in this sense of God the Father. But human religion is also characterized at many points by a much more mystical sense of the divine, welling up, as it were, from within – from within the whole cosmos or from within the human heart and mind. People refer here to an experienced sense of communion, even union, with the divine. The Judaeo-Christian tradition speaks in this sense of God as Spirit.

Two features distinguish the peculiarly Christian way of thinking of these two modes of divine presence and activity. One is that each of them is christologically determined. God the Father is known through his self-revelation in the Person and work of his incarnate Son. The character of God is shown in Jesus and nothing can be said of God the Father that contradicts the self-sacrificial love for other people – whether friends and followers, or the lost and the unloved, or even his enemies – that characterized the way of Jesus Christ. Similarly the Holy Spirit is as much the Spirit of Christ as of the Father and nothing can be said about the Spirit that contradicts the deeply personal and searching character of the love of God revealed in Jesus. This latter point will be recalled again and again as we attempt to specify the nature and activity of the Holy Spirit in later sections of this chapter.

The second feature that distinguishes the peculiarly Christian understanding of the Spirit is the one already stressed here and in chapter three; namely the distinct identity of the Spirit as a personal centre in God, related not only to creatures (as experience of the Spirit in all religions implies) but to the other two personal centres in God – the Father and the Son – so that fellowship and community are not only a product of the work of God as Spirit in the human world, but essential internal features of God's own life as the blessed and glorious Trinity.

THE GIVER OF LIFE

The Creed alternates at this point between phrases characterizing the divinity of the Holy Spirit and phrases indicating the Spirit's special role *vis-à-vis* creation. Of course, the title 'the Lord', as well as emphasizing the Spirit's divinity, refers also to the Spirit's role in relation to us humans. But we have to recall the sea-change that came over the notion of 'lord' when God's self-revelation in Jesus Christ discloses the nature of that 'lordship' as that of grace, service, friendship and love. No less can be said of the Spirit's lordship than was said above of the lordship of Jesus Christ. The title may indicate divinity, but the nature of the divine is very differently understood in the light of Christ.

But of course God does not cease to be God – the creator and upholder of our world – and the next phrase in the Creed picks out a special function that the Judaeo-Christian tradition attributes to the agency of God as Spirit, namely, 'the giver of life'. As with all divine activity, the other Persons of the Trinity are intimately involved in the gift of life, but it is the Spirit in particular that the Christian creeds affirm to be responsible for the phenomenon of life in the created world – for life and its evolution in the first place, and for new life, resurrection life, in the second great phase of God's creative plan.

There is a tendency in the Christian tradition to restrict the Spirit's life-giving work to the second of these two phases of creation, namely, the new creation, or recreation, that begins with the resurrection of Jesus Christ and its consequences for humankind. But the life-giving activity of the Spirit is, in fact, much wider than this. In a later section of this chapter, I shall consider the Creator Spirit – the Spirit's role in creation itself, the widest context of all for our understanding of the work of God as Spirit. In the last chapter, I spoke of the Spirit's role in all forms of human spirituality and creativity, and I shall return to this theme below. This is a much more specific function than that of creation, of course, though still less restricted and less exclusive than that of the inspiration of the explicit and self-conscious Christian Church. In between the wider and the narrower functions – the functions, that is, of creation and inspiration – we find a special place being given to the Spirit's role as life-giver.

Life is an extraordinary feature of the natural world. In chapter four, on creation, I have already expressed wonder at the capacity of the basic stuff of the world to complexify, through cosmic and biological evolution, into the manifold forms of life on this planet, culminating in the emergence of *homo sapiens*. This is a remarkable phenomenon on any account, but all the more so if, as many believe, the conditions for the evolution of life have only materialized once in this corner of this planetary system, within this galaxy; namely, here on Earth. Even the sceptical philosopher, David Hume, was led to postulate some vitalistic principle behind this ordered, complex, life-producing system. Hume, of course, thought of this principle as blind and impersonal, and many moderns have followed him; but, as was urged in chapter four, it is not, in fact, too difficult to discern an overall intention behind the evolution of ever more complex forms of life. And if there is any truth in our explanation of why the scheme of things inevitably permits much suffering and evil on the way to a future perfection, then there is good reason to stick to the intimations of purpose and thus personhood behind the life-producing world order.

But Christianity suggests more than simply a purpose behind the evolution of life. The world order may have a God-given *capacity* to evolve life, but so many apparent coincidences have to occur if ever that capacity is to be realized in the actual appearances in the universe of first life, then consciousness, then mind and personality, that it makes sense for Christians to suggest that the system needs a providential guiding hand. This is where the pervasive function of the Holy Spirit as giver of life comes in. It is not that we are postulating another form of the God of the gaps, referring to God, that is, in order to account for some particular features of the natural world believed to be entirely beyond the scope of scientific explanation. On the contrary, the evolutionary story can be told without reference to a vitalistic principle (or life-producing force) let alone to God. But the whole story is much more *intelligible* if the emergence of life and of the higher forms of life here on Earth is attributed to the intentional activity of the divine Spirit, permeating the whole web of natural energies and causes and drawing out their inbuilt potentialities. The life-giving Spirit, we may suppose, operates immanently and holistically within the creation, realizing its potentialities precisely in and through the story of cosmic and biological evolution, which, without such a guiding hand, seems well-nigh incredible. This is the broadest sense in which the Holy Spirit is the giver of life.

But it is to the second and much more particular sense of the Holy Spirit as the giver of life that we must now turn. Christians hold that the special gift of the Spirit which follows the resurrection of Jesus Christ from the dead makes available to the Christian Church and its members something of the power of the resurrection life – the new life promised to those who embrace God's forgiveness made known in Jesus Christ. It is the Spirit who energizes and, as we shall see, sanctifies those being caught up into the life of God through membership of Christ's 'body' – not just individually but corporately as the fellowship of Christians and through them, by anticipation, the whole human family. Of course all this is anticipation. For, while still on Earth, we are raised with Christ only metaphorically. Our literal resurrection is still to come. But something of the power of that literal resurrection which we await is made available here and now through the activity of the Holy Spirit in the lives of Christians and in the fellowship of the Church. There is a special spiritual resource and a special spiritual energy at work already in the human world.

The new life that the Spirit brings cannot be thought of in impersonal or irrational terms, as though some magical power has been made available to Christians. The Spirit is deeply personal. Indeed the Spirit is one of the Persons in God, the Holy Trinity. The Spirit is thoroughly rational, being the Spirit of Christ, the incarnate *Logos*, the Word by whom all things were made. Of course, the Spirit does operate at all levels of the human personality – not only through believers' minds but also through their hearts and affections – as well as in and through the corporate life of Christians. But if it is indeed the Spirit of Christ that we are talking about, we cannot speak of this divine power in any way that goes against the grace and the patience and the love that are revealed in Christ as God's way with the world.

To illustrate this point I will add a note about the relation between the new life bestowed and energized by the Holy Spirit and the gift of healing. For many Christians seem to expect the power of God's Spirit to work, even miraculously, to heal men and women from both mental and physical disease. We have to tread very carefully here. There is indeed a sense in which the Spirit brings wholeness and healing – integrating the physical, mental and spiritual lives of those who, by faith, allow themselves explicitly and consciously to become vehicles and instruments of God's work in the world. Such spiritual integrity often brings not only mental peace but physical well-being as well. Moreover, the faith of Christians, their prayers, and their Spirit-filled lives, may well have effects, by God's grace, on other people's mental and physical state. There is a Christian ministry of healing that complements the work of human medicine (which itself can become equally inspired and equally the vehicle of the Spirit's work). But Christians should be wary of the idea that the power of the Spirit operates directly, bypassing the conditions of our mortal life and overriding the God-given structures within which providence works and furthers the life-giving purposes of God. A christologically informed doctrine of the Spirit will not abandon the primacy of the way of the cross or go back on the specifically Christian insight that in the conditions of our earthly pilgrimage God's will is done and made known through suffering. Talk of the Spirit's power to heal can foster illusion and credulity if not controlled and schooled by genuinely Christian experience of the way God works to bring good out of evil. Evil and suffering are not abolished. They are overcome by the Spirit's bringing home to us and enlivening us with the power of Christ *crucified* and risen.

WHO PROCEEDS FROM THE FATHER [AND THE SON]

The next clause of the Nicene Creed reverts to pure theology and has become the most controversial of all. In the Western Churches we affirm that the Holy Spirit 'proceeds from the Father and the Son'. It is clear that this theological statement refers, not to the sending of the Spirit into the world or the Church, but rather to the inner trinitarian relations – the relations between the Persons in God prior to any activity *vis-à-vis* creatures. Now the Eastern Orthodox Churches object to the last phrase, 'and the Son' (*filioque* in Latin). This may well seem a pretty obscure dispute to the ordinary Christian, let alone to the outsider. But one thing is quite clear: as a matter of historical fact, this phrase was added to the ancient Creed of the universal Church in the year AD 589 by a unilateral decision of the Western Church. It is not surprising that the Orthodox object. For this reason alone, in our ecumenical age, where a reunion of east and west has become a matter of widespread concern and a real, if still remote, possibility, it is suggested that the phrase now be omitted from the Nicene Creed. That is why the new agreed translation – still, of course, a Western affair – puts it in square brackets. And we must surely agree that it should really be omitted, at least until such time as the genuinely universal Church of the future requests its reinstatement.

But this dispute is not simply a matter of history and present courtesy. Real theological differences lie behind the controversy, and these are much more difficult to handle. Indeed, theologically speaking, we may well have some doubts about both formulations, Eastern as well as Western. Of course, if we *were* talking about the bestowal of the Spirit upon creatures, a plausible case could be made for each formulation. Westerners could point out that Christ, the incarnate Son, promised that *he* would send 'another Comforter', and so the gift of the Spirit cannot be the Father's alone. Easterners could rejoin that Christ himself, at his baptism, *received* the Spirit, and so there remains a priority with the Father's action where this gift is concerned.

But these points are irrelevant to the actual case of *inner* trinitarian theology. Here our doubts over *both* formulations concern the priority given to the Father by both West and East. Easterners object to what they see as an asymmetrical Western linear view of the Spirit's 'procession' from the Father and the Son. They wish to affirm the more symmetrical view that the triune God is equally differentiated in the 'begetting' of the Son and the 'procession' of the Spirit. But both views retain an element of subordination regarding the second and third Persons of the Trinity. The Father is still being thought of as the fount of deity. And the Son and the Spirit are still being thought of as derived from the Father whether in linear, asymmetrical, fashion or not. But if we were right, in chapter three, to reject all forms of subordination and to insist that God just *is* a Trinity of Persons, the eternal 'processions' always involving mutual interpenetration and reciprocity so that the Father is never without the Son and the Spirit, the Son never without the Father and the Spirit, and the Spirit never without the Father and the Son, then certainly we shall want to reject any idea of linear asymmetrical derivation, but we shall also want to reject even symmetrical *derivation*. Even the Eastern version is suspect; for like the Western version, it retains the idea of proceeding *from*, where what is required is a more robust affirmation of mutual and reciprocal 'processions'.

Still, we cannot re-write the Creed. The best policy is to follow the Eastern Church in going back to the simpler affirmation of the undivided Church and supplement its very proper insistence on the absolute divinity of the Holy Spirit with the recognition that, in fact, all three Persons of the blessed and glorious Trinity 'proceed' both from and to each other.

WHO WITH THE FATHER AND THE SON IS WORSHIPPED AND GLORIFIED

There are no such problems with the next clause. The theme of the Spirit's divinity is sustained with the assertion that the Holy Spirit, with the Father and the Son, is worshipped and glorified. All three Persons of the divine Trinity are the natural and proper object of adoration and praise from creatures.

That God is to be worshipped and glorified is a natural and common motif in all theistic religion. Creatures acknowledge their status as creatures by responding to their Maker, Redeemer and Sustainer with worship and praise. Non-human creatures do this just by being what they are: 'I will consider my cat Jeoffrey', wrote the poet Christopher Smart, 'For he is the servant of the living God, duly and daily serving him. For at the first glance of the glory of God in the East he worships in his way. For this is done by wreathing his body seven times round with elegant quickness.' But humans, who can and do become aware of the God who made them and loves them and is preparing them for eternal beatitude, express their worship and adoration consciously, especially, as we shall see, in the liturgies and praises of the Church. Moreover, as was explained in chapter three, this whole process of explicit creaturely response is energized by the interior working of the Holy Spirit, so that worshippers, both individually and corporately, are being taken into the trinitarian life of God.

But the point being stressed at this stage in the Creed is that the Spirit is the proper object of human worship. God, in all three Persons, is to be glorified. The triune God is equally to be adored. This means that we cannot be too happy with the suggestion often made in western Christianity that Christian worship is, strictly speaking, addressed *to* the Father, *through* the Son and *in* the Spirit. There is some truth in this formulation, obviously. For the incarnate Son, into whose risen 'body' we are being adopted and incorporated, is indeed the one mediator between God the Father and ourselves. Through him we come to know God as our Father in heaven. And, as repeatedly emphasized in this chapter, our prayers and worship do take place in the Spirit, as we are caught up by the indwelling Spirit into God. But none of this can be allowed to override the recognition, expressed quite clearly here in the Creed, that Father, Son and Holy Spirit are all, equally and together, to be worshipped and glorified. For, although we can and must address God as our Father, we cannot think of isolating God the Father from God the Son or God the Holy Spirit. The God whom we know as Father is, most basically, Father, Son and Holy Spirit, the glorious and undivided Trinity.

WHO HAS SPOKEN THROUGH THE PROPHETS

Turning back to the special activities of God, the Holy Spirit, in the world, the Creed now focuses on the function of inspiration, and, in particular, the inspiration of the prophets of old.

More will be said about inspiration in general later in this chapter. But the very special activity of the Spirit in the inspiration of the Old Testament prophets is what is singled out for particular mention here. Once again we must beware of crude, quasi-magical, ideas of the prophets being nothing but passive instruments of direct divine dictation. That is not how God operates in the world. Nonetheless, the prophets of ancient Israel do have a unique place in the formation of the faith and the community that were to provide the human context of the incarnation, and what the Creed is drawing attention to here is the providential work of God's Holy Spirit in preparing that context and creating the special conditions in which the divine Son could indeed take our nature upon him and come amongst us as one of us. The meaning and purpose of this incarnation have been explained in chapters

five and six. We are now being asked to ponder the mystery
of prophetic inspiration which played so central a role in
fashioning the human social and religious context for the
coming of the Christ.

We may extend the discussion at this point to consider
again the place of Holy Scripture in the Christian scheme of
things. For what has been said about the inspiration of the
prophets applies also, if perhaps less vividly, to the inspiration
of the law books and the histories and the wisdom writings
that with the prophetic books make up the Hebrew Bible and
even more centrally, so Christians hold, to the inspiration of
the Gospel authors, the historian of Acts, the letter writers
and the visionary prophet, whose writings make up the New
Testament, the human witness to the story of Jesus Christ and
its immediate consequences. As was pointed out in chapter
one, all these are purely human, fallible, witnesses. But the
Spirit not only inspires them; he also uses them to bring
home to us the story of Jesus Christ. The book consisting of
their writings – the Bible – becomes the Word of God to us,
as the Spirit who inspired them inspires us with insight into
its true meaning and indeed lays claim to our lives as Christians. So there is a double sense in which the Holy Spirit has
spoken through the prophets. They were enabled by the
Spirit to advance in leaps and bounds in understanding God's
purposes and nature. And we are enabled by the Spirit to
appropriate their message – and that of their successors who
bore witness to God's culminating self-revelation in the incarnate one. Divine special providence is at work not only in the
incarnation itself, but in its preparation through the history
of Israel and Israel's faith, in which the prophets played so
crucial a part, and in the all-too-human witness to the story of
Jesus Christ himself. Ultimately, so Christians believe, it is the
Holy Spirit of God who brings all this about and brings its
meaning home to us.

CREATOR SPIRIT

I now attempt to fill out Christian understanding of the
Holy Spirit beyond the aspects, internal and external, actually
mentioned in the Creed. And first I go back to the widest

and most universal of the Spirit's external functions, namely that of creation itself. As already emphasized, all three Persons of the Trinity are involved in the process of creation. God the Father, by a free act of supreme creativity, posits the fundamental substance of the world in being. But he does not act alone. The divine Son or Word, eternally destined to become incarnate in this created world, determines its rational and eventual personal nature as a world that can reflect back images of the divine in communities of persons. And the Holy Spirit, immanently pervading the whole created cosmos, actually fulfils God's creative plan by drawing out its God-given potentialities from within. I have already touched on the work of the indwelling Creator Spirit in eliciting the phenomenon of life. But the Spirit's creative energies are more basic and more pervasive than that. I refer once more to the book of Genesis at the beginning of the Hebrew Bible, which captures something of this all-embracing presence and power with its vivid image of the spirit of God 'hovering over the surface of the waters' (Genesis 1.2).

The immanent Spirit draws out, in and through the processes of cosmic and biological evolution, and within both the natural and the human worlds, all the possibilities – of which life is the most fundamental – that exist within creation. Its beauty, its novelty, its derivative creativity, but especially its evolution of persons in relation, are all aspects of the Spirit's work in creation. And as the creation becomes responsive to God in conscious and explicit ways through humanity's emergence into the spiritual dimension, so the way is opened up for the Spirit's further activity in redemption and new creation, of which I have already spoken. Thus, the personal and interpersonal products of God's whole creative process are drawn back into the life of God through the Spirit's further, recreative, agency.

INSPIRATION

Mention has already been made of the inspiration of the prophets and the further inspiration of those for whom the inspired Scriptures become the Word of God. But there are more widespread forms of inspiration than these. All moral vision, artistic skill and scientific discovery and invention are, ultimately speaking, gifts from God. It is the Spirit who inspires and energizes all goodness, beauty and truth in the human world. So, as with the creative and the life-giving work of the Spirit, inspiration has a wider and a narrower scope. The phenomena of goodness, beauty and truth in the world are marks of the Spirit's wider activity, and this often occurs at levels below that of consciousness. Or at least the people thus inspired are often not aware that it is the Spirit of God who is eliciting their moral, aesthetic or scientific insight. I have already touched on the narrower, much more self-conscious, sphere of the Spirit's activity in and through believers who explicitly open up their lives to the Spirit, in speaking of prophecy. The same is true of all other special vocations (and, of course, all vocations are special!) and all specifically religious and Christian forms of life.

I might insert a word here about what differentiates the Old Testament prophets and the authors of the Scriptures, Old and New, from the equally inspired lives of Christian (and other) saints down the ages. It is not something distinctive about the manner or degree of inspiration that energizes the biblical writers compared, say, with the saints of the Christian Church. What makes the biblical writers, including the prophets, special is their providential role *vis-à-vis* the salvation history to which the books of the Bible bear witness. The special, indeed unique, events concerning Jesus Christ and the preparation for his coming are what give those writings their special place in Christianity. But their inspired authors are fallible human beings just like any other inspired men and women through whom the Holy Spirit works the works of God.

After all, there are other and later prophets than those of the Bible. As we shall see, St Paul lists prophecy as one of the gifts of the Spirit. There are twentieth-century Christian prophets, like Reinhold Niebuhr, the American social ethicist and critic of all political absolutisms, or Trevor Huddleston, the critic of apartheid in South Africa during the 1950s and 1960s, and many others, whose insight into moral and spiritual realities and whose boldness in proclaiming the moral truth as they saw it were undoubtedly prophetic and inspired.

Neither biblical nor post-biblical prophecy, incidentally, is a matter of some quasi-magical, or even God-given, ability to predict the future. As we saw in chapter four, God is fashioning a genuinely open created world, whose future is not fixed in advance and cannot therefore be predicted in detail (whatever predestinarians may say). Prophecy, rather, is a matter of inspired insight into the realities of human life, both personal and corporate. The prophet is enabled to see into the human heart and to warn contemporaries of where things are heading and of what is likely to happen if they do not repent and mend their ways.

THE GIFTS OF THE SPIRIT

Let us turn explicitly to the theme of the gifts and fruit of the Spirit, with which, among New Testament authors, St Paul was much preoccupied, and which have become again a matter of central concern in contemporary Christian circles. In this context we are certainly restricting our interest to the narrower, more explicit and specific effects of the working of God as Spirit, subsequent to Christ's resurrection, as Christians and the Church are empowered with something of the new 'risen' life that one day will be fully ours in heaven. In this section we consider the *gifts* of the Spirit. (The distinction between the gifts and the fruit of the Spirit is somewhat arbitrary and Paul himself blurs it. But we can take *gifts* to mean special – and very diverse – gifts that different members of the Christian body find themselves endowed with, and *fruit* to mean the characteristic virtues and attitudes that life in the Spirit is supposed to evoke in all Christians.)

At different times in Christian history and in different contexts, very different features of life in the 'body' of Christ are singled out as special gifts of the Spirit. Priorities undoubtedly change and no one who is sensitive to the conditions and pressures of the modern world will be content simply to reiterate St Paul's list of spiritual gifts in 1 Corinthians 12. A critical approach to Scripture will enable us to recognize the embeddedness of Paul's discernments and discriminations in the cultural and religious conditions of his day as well as in the particular problems of the Corinthian

Church which he had in view. Clearly there will be a family resemblance between his priorities and ours, but our list is bound to differ from his.

Before we examine the variety of spiritual gifts we should consider one which Christians hold to be pre-eminently the effect of the Holy Spirit's working in the community as a whole, namely, fellowship – *koinonia* in Greek; the special kind of mutually supportive Christian fellowship that, in principle and hopefully in practice, results from our adoption into the 'body' of Christ on Earth. More will be said about this in the next section and in the next chapter; but clearly, if we are being fashioned into the likeness of the God who is Trinity, then fellowship, mutuality and reciprocity are of the essence of Christianity, and no treatment of the Spirit's gifts can be content with purely individual skills and powers. As Paul himself makes clear, it is a test of any purported spiritual gift whether or not it contributes to the body's harmony.

But now for the variety of gifts: we have already spoken of prophecy – one of Paul's own list – and in the sense defined above, prophecy must indeed be valued as a gift of the Spirit, if we are serious about the Church's task in helping individuals and nations to face up to the truth about themselves and to the implications for good or ill of their actions and policies.

Paul's stress on wisdom and knowledge, and elsewhere on the importance of teachers in the Church, can also be taken over as indicators of the lasting Christian conviction that, as St John puts it, the Spirit will lead us into all truth. The Church needs teachers – and that includes theologians – if the truth of the gospel is to be understood and appropriated wisely and related to contemporary knowledge and contemporary problems.

Preaching is also a special gift and a special vocation. Not all Christians are called or enabled to preach the good news with discernment and discrimination. Moreover, we should not expect the gift of powerful preaching to bypass the necessity of training and discipline in the Church's seminaries – training not least in how to study the Bible critically and interpret it realistically and with genuine insight. As is God's way with the world in general, the Spirit works through the co-operative efforts of those engaged in the training of preachers and indeed of all other aspects of training for the ministry. For there are many gifts of ministry, besides the gift of preaching. Different people excel in pastoral, liturgical and contemplative skills. I shall return to these matters in the next chapter, on the Church.

Reference may be made again here to the healing ministry – a genuine gift of the Spirit, but one which needs to be fostered with great care and awareness of the possibilities of false expectations, as was argued above.

All these gifts concern a variety of leadership roles that different individuals may be called upon to play in the Christian body. Of course, the phenomenon of particular individuals finding themselves possessed of powerful and authoritative leadership skills is not peculiar to the Christian Church. It is interesting that sociologists have borrowed a Christian term to single out the fact of 'charismatic' leadership generally; for the word *charisma* is the Greek for 'a gift of grace'. But not all charismatic leadership is God-inspired. The psychological – and sociological – factors that make for special powers and skills in leading others can be put to evil and perverse use. Whether or not such powers are God-inspired must be judged, in general, by their contribution to the causes of goodness, beauty and truth, and, in particular, by their contribution to the harmony and outreach of the Christian Church.

The so-called 'charismatic movement' in the churches of today has tended to single out extraordinary experiences of enthusiasm or ecstasy by individuals or groups in the Christian fellowship as special gifts of the Spirit or manifestations of the Spirit's activity. A warning note on this has already been sounded in chapter two, when we were reflecting on experience of God. There are indeed special manifestations of the Spirit's power and activity in the Church where believers find new resources of joy and peace in believing, new insight, and new enthusiasm in life and liturgy and in bearing witness to the truths of God. But to see some special significance in paranormal phenomena like speaking in tongues is probably unwise. Paul himself, in an age and a culture where such things were more widespread (and their psychology not at all understood) was surprisingly wary of giving them undue significance (see 1 Corinthians 14). And as for more

extreme manifestations, such as the so-called 'Toronto blessing', mature Christians are best advised to have nothing to
do with them. The Holy Spirit of God and of Christ, who
searches the depths of the heart and endows men and women
in Christ's 'body' with the gifts of fellowship, discernment
and love, is hardly to be discerned in such irrational and
impersonal phenomena.

If I have written somewhat sharply of the charismatic
movement, it is because of its tendency to go along not only
with biblical fundamentalism but with a somewhat credulous
interest in the paranormal. Christians should not think of the
Spirit's 'power' as specially evident in such phenomena. We
have schooled ourselves, rather, to see the power of God in
the weakness of the cross, in the way God brings good out
of evil, and in the way the Holy Spirit builds up Christian
fellowship and forms Christian character – as we shall see in
the next section on the fruit of the Spirit. Moreover there is
a dark side to the charismatic movement – its unwise espousal
of belief in demon possession and the practice of exorcism.
The authentic Christian gospel frees us not only from the
'powers' that bind us, but from belief in their independent,
personal, reality, as will be clear to anyone who has followed
and accepted the reasons I gave, in chapter four, for treating
talk of devils as mythology.

One other alleged spiritual gift, mentioned by Paul in 1
Corinthians 12, has not been acknowledged here, and that is
the working of miracles. This too must be assessed in the light
of what was said in chapter four about the way God works in
the world by providence rather than by miracle; that is to say,
mediately, in and through the lives and deeds and words of
those who love him, and in and through the circumstances of
their lives. In another sense of the word 'miracle', as already
acknowledged, there are indeed miracles of grace in the lives
of the saints and wherever good is brought out of evil.

THE FRUIT OF THE SPIRIT

The effects of the working of the Holy Spirit in the lives and
in the fellowship of Christians is spelled out by St Paul in his
repeated lists of virtues and qualities which he expects to

see in those being conformed to Christ and drawn into the
trinitarian life of God. They reflect the 'power' of the resurrection at work already in the Church on Earth, as Christians
are gradually being energized and transformed by the Holy
Spirit into the divine likeness.

'Love, joy, peace, patience, kindness, goodness, fidelity,
gentleness, and self-control': that is Paul's list in Galatians
5.22. In some ways it is a pretty standard list of the virtues
constitutive of good character. Similar lists occur in other
religions and in the writings of secular moralists. And indeed,
wherever such virtues are found, Christians will attribute
them ultimately to the wider, more universal, working of
God's Holy Spirit in the world. Not that such virtues are often
actually found, least of all in the ancient world in which
Christian character – and Christian fellowship – tended to
stand out as something very special, rather more than it does
today when Christians themselves are, I am afraid, likely to be
influenced, even corrupted, by less positive, worldly, values.
And saintly character, manifesting these characteristics as a
whole over a lifetime is a very rare phenomenon. But, in any
case, specifically Christian character, energized by the Spirit
of Christ crucified and risen, is not fully captured by lists
such as these. There is something more special, more Christ-
like, in the way in which these virtues are manifested in a
genuinely Spirit-filled Christian life. This is clear from Paul's
great hymn to love in 1 Corinthians 13. Here, in verses 4–8,
the priority of love and its Christ-like nature are spelled out
in unforgettable words:

Love is patient and kind. Love envies no one, is never
boastful, never conceited, never rude; love is never selfish,
never quick to take offence. Love keeps no score of wrongs,
takes no pleasure in the sins of others, but delights in the
truth. There is nothing love cannot face; there is no limit
to its faith, its hope, its endurance. Love will never come to
an end.

It is to be noted how this chapter, insisting on the primacy of
love, relativizes all the gifts of the Spirit previously mentioned. Such love is the test of whether the more diverse gifts
are indeed gifts of God.

But lists of virtues and descriptions of the nature and centrality of love, important as they are in trying to capture the
character of Christian lives being recreated by the Holy Spirit
into the image and likeness of God, are still being given in
very general terms. The most they do is to spell out something
of the family resemblance that ought to be discernible in the
members of the 'body' of Christ on Earth. They do not, however, capture the individuality of sainthood, the special and
unique 'character' that each Christian is in his or her own life
both as a human and as a Christian personality. This uniqueness is partly the result of the combination of the general
virtues, including that of love, with the diverse special gifts
that distinguish one member of the 'body' from the others.
And it is partly the result of the unique history of interpersonal relations which each Christian has with other members
of the 'body' and particularly with Jesus Christ himself. This
is what talk of being taken into God means. In each case, and
in very different ways, the Holy Spirit enables the Christian to
grow in grace, not only through Christian discipleship, but
also through life-long communion with his or her risen Lord.

So far, this exposition of specifically Christian understanding of the fruit of the Spirit has been carried out in individualistic terms – in terms, that is, of Christian character and
Christian characters. But we must not forget that personality
is a relational matter. The virtues we have been discussing are
realized in interpersonal relation. And sainthood is a product
not just of the Spirit's work upon a particular life, not even
a Christ-centred and Christ-related life. It is a product of
membership of the Christian community, the 'body' of Christ
on Earth, the Church. Christian character and Christian characters alike are fashioned in the context of the fellowship –
the *koinonia* – which, as we saw in the last section, has the
primacy among the gifts of the Spirit, just as love has the primacy in the Spirit's fruit.

SANCTIFICATION

It follows that, as we turn to consider the work of the Spirit
under its traditional name of 'sanctification', we must give as
much attention to the corporate dimension as to the individual.

As pointed out in chapter five, sanctification is the second
and long-term stage of the process of salvation initiated by
the incarnation. By his life and teaching and by his deeds,
culminating in his death on the cross, Jesus, God incarnate,
enacts and reveals the costly divine forgiveness and wins our
response of penitence and commitment. But the actual remak-
ing of our lives – our transformation into the divine likeness
– is achieved by God the Holy Spirit, sent into our hearts and
into our midst, to energize us with the power of Christ's resurrection and build us up into a fellowship that, as it is taken
into God, comes gradually to mirror the divine fellowship,
the Trinity. This is the process known as sanctification –
making holy, refashioning God's wayward human creatures
into saints and into anticipations of the communion of saints.

We see the effects of this process in individual Christian
lives, in the Christian community, the Church, and, to some
extent, in human society more widely.

All that was said in the previous section about the fruit of
the Spirit really concerned the first of these aspects of sanctification – the Spirit's activity in forming Christian character,
as individual men and women are made more Christ-like and
schooled in the Christian virtues. The second aspect of sanctification – the Spirit's activity in fashioning forms of Christian
fellowship that bear witness to God's saving grace and embody
its corporate effect in the common life of Christians – will be
treated more fully in the next chapter on the Church. Here
we must concentrate on the third aspect of sanctification –
the Spirit's activity in transforming the whole human world.

This is the most difficult aspect to handle. It is not surprising that some Christians think of the saints and the Church
as islands or fortresses of grace in a basically godless world.
They may constitute beacons of light, but their function is
to draw people out of an alienated world into specifically
Christian communities, where alone God's ideal future is
anticipated. But this is not how the mainstream churches
have seen the social task and the social effectiveness of the
Christian gospel.

To spell out the social implications of Christianity for
society at large, not just for the Christian communities themselves, is to engage in Christian social ethics – an aspect of

Christian reflection and teaching that has acquired increasing emphasis and commitment, in both Catholic and Protestant circles, in the course of the nineteenth and twentieth centuries. Of course, there are plenty of earlier examples of Christian concern with the structures of society at large, but, apart from the extreme millenarian movements which have prophesied and sometimes tried to implement the most radical transformations of society, the Churches were generally inclined to emphasize the stabilizing factors of family, law and good government as falling within the providence of God for the good of all. But, with greater and greater recognition of the extent of poverty, injustice and oppression in the world, the Churches have applied themselves increasingly to the task of spelling out and working for the necessary changes that are required if God's will is really to be done on Earth as it is in heaven. The ethics of the kingdom of God – the application of the love commandment to all that makes for human well-being – has been proclaimed in terms of what the World Council of Churches calls a 'just, participatory and sustainable society', and we have seen the development, in our time, of political theologies, including liberation theologies, concerned to work for a more just world, a fairer distribution of the world's resources, and freedom from poverty and oppression.

It is interesting to note that the Churches have grown in realism where these matters are concerned. On the one hand they have come to recognize the unwisdom of embracing utopian schemes for total revolutionary transformation that would repeat all the errors and horrors of communism. On the other hand, they have also come to recognize that it is a mistake to think of the 'idea of a Christian society', as though the whole world could be reconstructed solely and explicitly on Christian principles. Christians have learned to work with men and women of other faiths or none for a more just world which, while being conformed more and more to the will of God revealed in Jesus Christ, nevertheless – and necessarily – includes both tolerance of and respect for other religious and ethical views. This makes sense, given our earlier recognition of the wider, more universal, scope of the Holy Spirit's activity wherever truth, beauty and goodness are being discerned or striven for.

All the same, our interest in the sanctification of the world will lead us to enquire, not only about Christian social ethical theory, but also about the degree of actual transformation that the human world has undergone throughout the so-called Christian centuries. For, despite what has just been said about the wider scope of the Spirit's activity, if the power of the resurrection has indeed been released into the world, there should be signs of its special effectiveness not only in transformed Christian lives and new communities of grace, but also in the gradual betterment and unification of the whole human world.

There is much understandable disillusion about the idea of progress in world history, given the unspeakable horrors of tyranny, genocide and war experienced in our own century. The pervasive, recurrent, fact of human sin can easily obscure the signs of God's patient, providential re-ordering of human life, at the social as well as at the individual level. But the fact remains that Christian values have made their mark on the way in which democratic constitutions, international organizations and policies of co-operation, and universal respect for human rights have tended to prevail in the long run, despite all the setbacks and disappointments of which the media make us continually aware. In our own time, the ecological movement, working for the conservation of, and respect for, our whole natural environment, can be seen as a further manifestation of the Spirit's sanctifying work.

It is sometimes said that these, more enlightened, aspects of the modern world are products of the secular rather than the religious consciousness. But this ignores the fact that modern secular humanism is itself a product of the Christian centuries. Take respect for human rights, for example. This only makes sense in a basically Christian context, where the value of each human life is founded on its status as that of a child of God, destined for eternity. And the excessive individualism, even selfishness, of much secular insistence on one's rights is best countered by recognition of the reciprocity of rights and responsibilities in the community of those made in the image of God.

Similar comments could be made on the increasing provision of education and health care, on the abolition of slavery and of the death penalty, on the democratization of human institutions at every level, and on the charters governing international organizations. Even where these have been thoroughly secularized, they rest on a Christian foundation, and their distortions and perversions are best overcome by a recovery of their fundamentally religious motivation.

All in all, then, a case can still be made for reading world history in terms of progress. In the providence of God, the Christian west – for this has largely been a European phenomenon – has been instrumental to the Holy Spirit's work of global unification and sanctification. Of course, the story is immensely ambivalent and there is a long way to go – but this is true at every level; at those of the individual and the Church, as well as that of society at large – wherever the Holy Spirit works through all-too-human, fallible, human media.

EXPERIENCE OF THE SPIRIT

In conclusion, we return to the subject of our experience of the Holy Spirit, concentrating now on conscious, explicit, awareness of the reality of God as Spirit, active in us, in other people, in the Church and in the world. For there are two sides to what we mean by 'experience'. There is the subjective, inner, sense of the realities with which we have to do. And there are the objective, outer, facts which we experience and become aware of through lived encounter. It will be clear from all that has been said in this chapter that, in both senses, experience of the Spirit is virtually always mediated, whether by a sense of joy, or of conviction, or of being caught up in the praises and worship of the Church, or by something new and wonderful in the lives of Christian people whom we meet in the fellowship of the Church, or else by some breakthrough in the wider life of humankind as good is brought out of evil or an unjust social order overcome. The transition from apartheid to a multiracial democratic order in South Africa has, for many Christians there and here, been a striking example of the way in which God's recreative and transforming power does take effect in the world against all expectation. To have experienced that in our time is to have experienced something of the Spirit's sanctifying power.

Experience of the Spirit, then, is not, for most of us at least, a matter of extraordinary or paranormal ecstasies. It is a matter of deep, personal, awareness of the recreative power of God in our own lives, in the lives of other Christians (though not only these), and in the struggle for – and sometimes the achievement of – a better human world.

CHAPTER EIGHT

Church

WE BELIEVE IN THE CHURCH

It is rather strange, at this stage in the Creed, after lengthy profession of belief in the triune God and in God's creative, revelatory and reconciling action in the world, to find ourselves professing belief in the Church. For we do not have faith in the Church in the same way in which we have faith in God. Certainly, the Church is the object of belief of a very different kind from God the Father, God the Son and God the Holy Spirit. Indeed, the language of belief gives way to the language of acknowledgement and expectation in the last two clauses of the Creed: 'We acknowledge one baptism for the forgiveness of sins. We look for the resurrection of the dead, and the life of the world to come.'

Notwithstanding this shift in the meaning of belief and this move away from the language of belief to that of acknowledgement and hope, the fact remains that the Church, its sacraments and its future hope belong to the essence of Christianity. In the last three chapters of this book, I shall try to explain why this is so.

Belief in the Church is a matter of conviction that to be a Christian is to belong to the fellowship of those who are being conformed to Christ and adopted into his mystical 'body' through the inspiration and indwelling of God's Holy Spirit. Christianity, despite its stress on personal discipleship and personal holiness, is not an individualistic religion. Fellowship in an ordered community, with shared structures of worship and service, belongs to the very heart of Christianity. We have already emphasized the central Christian insight that the

image of God in humanity is itself a matter of persons in relation; and the renewed image, the divine likeness, into which
the Holy Spirit is refashioning those who respond to God's
saving grace, is essentially a corporate affair – eventually the
perfected communion of saints in heaven. The New Testament
is full of corporate imagery – the vine into which we are being
grafted as new branches, the body into which we are being
adopted and whose different members we become, each with
our own function *vis-à-vis* the harmony of the whole. You
simply cannot have an isolated Christian. To be a Christian is
to be a member of the 'body' of Christ on Earth.

Sometimes the Church is spoken of, rather extravagantly,
as 'an extension of the incarnation'. The logic behind this idea
is this: Christ, too, is not an isolated individual. His relations
with his mother, with his friends and disciples, and with those
adopted into his risen 'body' for all eternity, are part of his
identity. If Christ is God incarnate, then the Church, consisting of those united with him, becomes an extension of that
incarnation. But this is probably not a wise way of putting the
matter. It makes for confusion when we try to speak more
precisely of the divinity of Christ. As argued in chapter five,
Christ's divinity consists in the way in which God the Son is
the ultimate subject of *his* life. God the Son is not the subject
of our lives, even when we are united with the risen Christ
in his 'body' the Church. For similar reasons we will not be
too happy with the Eastern notion of 'divinization' for the
process whereby Christians and the Church are taken into the
trinitarian life of God by the Holy Spirit's sanctifying power.
We remain creatures and children of God by adoption, not by
nature.

In any case, we do not have to think of the Church as a
narrow and exclusive body, consisting solely of those who are
fully conscious of, and fully responsive to, the divine realities
considered so far in this book. We saw how the effectiveness
of what Christ did extends far beyond the sphere of those
who have explicitly embraced that revelation of the divine
love. And we saw how the Spirit of God and of Christ is at
work in the world in wider and more universal ways in the
whole history of religion and ethics, as well as in the ways

opened up by explicit Christian response, although even there extending beyond the self-awareness of Christians and the Church into the permeation of society itself by Christian values. All this means that we are quite justified in speaking of a hidden, implicit, Church as well as of the conscious, explicitly structured, Church which affirms the creeds, orders worship and claims the allegiance of committed Christians.

In any case, even the conscious, explicitly structured, Church consists of people at very different stages in their spiritual journeys and with very different degrees of commitment. It is self-defeating and no true witness to the all-embracing love of God, if Christians are exclusive and intolerant in laying down strict conditions of membership of the 'body'. There is a sense in which anyone attracted by the figure of Christ or by the fellowship and/or the worship of the Church can be regarded and welcomed as a member. And even the most committed of Christians are still only part-way there, still liable to fall back and manifest the most unchristian attitudes. The Church on Earth is very much a mixture of saints and sinners, and the saints are always partly sinners too. And the levels and degrees of understanding possessed by different members of the Church vary enormously. People have to be given room to grow and mature in understanding at their own pace and in their own time.

All this suggests the impropriety of trying to lay down rigid boundaries where membership of the 'body' of Christ on Earth is concerned. Of course there are limits to what the Church can tolerate. It cannot tolerate flagrant evil and injustice in its midst, but that is another matter. And, as we shall see, it is only reasonable to expect greater levels of commitment and understanding from those called to special forms of office and ministry in the Church. But the Church itself is open-ended and inclusive rather than exclusive, and, at this stage of God's creative plan, it is inevitably fuzzy at the edges.

It follows from this that much of what I now go on to discuss regarding the Church's nature will be somewhat idealistic. This is certainly true of the four traditional characteristics or 'notes' of the Church which the Creed lists in saying that we believe in 'one holy catholic and aspostolic' Church.

ONE

It may seem wildly unrealistic to proclaim the Church's unity when everyone knows how divided the empirical Church actually is. The empirical Church – that is, the Church as we experience it in history and at the present time – is split into numerous denominations. The first major division – that between the Western and the Eastern Churches – came to a head in AD 1054. In the west, the sixteenth-century Reformation saw the Lutheran and Calvinist and, in its own way, the Anglican, Churches breaking away from Rome. Many other Protestant subdivisions followed. And the later missionary movements transplanted these divisions in the Church of Christ all over the world. It is true that the twentieth century has witnessed a remarkable coming together of the Churches in the ecumenical movement of our time. But even where Christians have rediscovered the great deal that they have in common, most of the major denominations, to say nothing of the more sectarian splinter groups, remain out of communion with one another.

All the same, the unity of the Church is not only a visionary ideal and a future hope. There is an underlying unity despite the historical divisions, in so far as every Christian person and every Christian community are to some degree united with the one Lord Jesus Christ. The Spirit's work of creating and building up the one communion of saints goes on despite the weakness and the sinfulness of individuals and despite the perverseness and intransigence of the denominations. The empirical divisions are relatively superficial compared with these common spiritual bonds.

Moreover, the ecumenical movement, even empirically speak ing, has enabled Christian men and women from all the divided traditions and communities to become much more conscious of what they have in common – the Bible, the creeds handed down from the undivided Church, treasuries of liturgy and praise, the musical, artistic and architectural heritage of the Christian centuries, and the future hope of a purified and truly reunited world-wide Christian fellowship. It has become much more possible for Christians from different traditions to work together, pray together, and, increasingly, to sit lightly to the official barriers that inhibit intercommunion.

Even the Roman Catholic Church, at its Second Vatican Council, spoke of members of other Christian communions being in 'a certain, albeit imperfect, communion with the Catholic Church'.

It is also true that Christians have become much more aware of the inevitability, indeed the positive value, of plurality and creative disagreement *within* the one 'body' of Christ. It is recognized that the world-wide Christian Church, with its two thousand year history and long traditions of practice and belief, expressed in very different cultural and social conditions, is bound to contain much diversity and that this need not prevent us from working and praying together. Moreover, the variety of belief and practice within any one of the major Christian communions, including the Roman Catholic Church, is often as great as that between the different denominations. This underlines the possibility of discerning and accepting a fundamental unity in diversity.

Of course, there are, again, limits to what can count as membership of the one Church, even on the most liberal interpretation. (We are not thinking here of the hidden 'anonymous' Church in which the faithful of all religions and moralities can be claimed to participate.) The ecumenical movement can hardly be expected, officially, to endorse even such admirable bodies as the Unitarians and the Quakers, who explicitly reject central doctrines of the Creed, let alone such extreme heterodox movements as the Jehovah's Witnesses (who interpret the Bible quite wildly and despise the mainstream Churches) or the Mormons (who claim another revelation and another scripture). No, the oneness of the Church is the oneness of those who confess Jesus Christ as God and Saviour, and accept the historic creeds, such as the one which I am trying to expound. This unity is, in essence, the unity of those indwelt by the one Spirit, those being conformed to our one Lord Jesus Christ, and those being drawn into the love of the one eternal God.

HOLY

Similar remarks must be made about the second of the characteristics or 'notes' with which the Creed identifies the

Church. The Church of God is 'holy'. This might well seem just as implausible a claim as the claim that the Church is 'one'. As was pointed out in the first chapter of this book, one of the commonest objections to Christian belief comes from the fact that, far from fostering the holiness and fellowship and love that are supposed to flow from life in the Spirit, the Churches have been responsible for the wars of religion, persistent inter-communal hostilities and much persecution and intolerance, Christian leaders have often abused positions of power and responsibility, and many Christians have shown self-deception and sometimes the spirit of hatred and revenge. There is no denying or excusing these scandalous facts of Christian history and practice. And their victims are not easily going to see that the heart of the matter lies elsewhere.

But the heart of the matter does lie elsewhere. From one point of view the Christian Churches are indeed large-scale human institutions, with long histories and many millions of members. They have exercised a huge influence on the history of the world. It is not surprising that, like all human institutions, they have a dark side, calling for unequivocal condemnation, repentance and reform. But it should be possible to see that their participation in the story of human failures does not belong to their essence; for from another point of view – and this must be the decisive point of view when we are considering the theology of the Church – the Christian Church, in its fully explicit form, is a divine institution. In its essence, it consists of those who are being conformed to Christ and united with him in a Spirit-inspired and energized community, whose internal fellowship and outward service and care reflect something of the eternal love of God. The Church is holy just because it is the principal vehicle and instrument of the Holy Spirit's sanctifying work in the world. Despite its all-too-human fallibility, the Church – along with God's ancient people, the Jews – is the people of God on Earth. It is holy because the holy God is making God's people holy.

This theological perception of the Church's essential character would, of course, be hopelessly idealistic and unconvincing if there were no empirical signs of the effectiveness of the Holy Spirit's sanctifying work in Christian individuals and Church communities. But, as was pointed out in the last chapter, there is plenty of evidence, throughout history and today, for the actuality of holiness in the Christian Church. We think first of the saints – those remarkable Christian men and women whose sanctity shines out for all to see; St Benedict, St Francis, St Teresa of Avila, Mother Julian of Norwich, St Ignatius Loyola, to name but a few. And in all the Churches, there have been outstanding examples of selfless dedication to the care of the poor and the sick, of orphans and the aged. There have been innumerable missionaries and martyrs, who have spent themselves and given their lives, out of love for Christ and for all God's children. But we need not think only of outstanding individuals such as these. Every Christian will be aware of many ordinary people who have been an inspiration to them in their own spiritual journey, men and women unsung and unpublicized, in whom something of the grace and love of God is clearly discernible, often despite adversity, and whose faithfulness helps to sustain one's own Christian commitment. Sometimes what impresses is the quality of selfless love manifested in the deeds and attitudes of these people, and sometimes it is their evident spirituality, as practitioners of contemplative prayer. One of the myths prevalent in the contemporary religious world is that deep spirituality is more a product of the east – of Hinduism and Buddhism – than of the Christian west. But this betrays an astonishing ignorance not only of the spiritual classics of the Christian tradition, but also of the way in which, in every generation, that tradition enables people to discover for themselves the secret of prayer, meditation and contemplation.

But the actuality of holiness is not discerned solely in the dedicated and prayerful lives of individuals. As befits the trinitarian faith of Christians, holiness is perhaps most evident in the communal practices of prayer and worship that we find throughout the Christian world. They are most sharply focused, of course, in the monastic or quasi-monastic life of the many religious orders that exist within all the major strands of Christianity. Whether we think of Bec or Burford, Taizé or Iona, the reality and attraction of the spirituality of religious communities, often sustained and deepened, through association, by the places hallowed by their presence over many generations, are among the most tangible signs of the Church's holiness.

I shall return to this topic when considering the Church's worship in a later section of this chapter; for this communal dimension to the Church's holiness is not only evident in the special religious orders and communities that have graced Christian history, but also in the regular liturgical life of cathedrals, churches and chapels all over the Christian world. At Christmas and in Holy Week and at Easter – but also throughout the Church's year – innumerable congregations experience for themselves something of the Church's unity and holiness.

CATHOLIC

The word 'catholic' means 'universal' or 'world-wide' and this third characteristic or 'note' of the Christian Church refers to the fact, which in this case is both theological and empirical, that the Church is not a tribal, local or national body, but an unrestricted, universal communion open to the whole of humanity. And indeed its membership and its manifold structured organizations extend all over the globe. This is obviously the case with the Roman Catholic Church, but the term 'catholic' cannot possibly be restricted to that – albeit the largest – denomination. The whole 'catholic' Church, despite its empirical divisions, consists of all Christian bodies willing to think of themselves as branches of the universal Church. Membership of the World Council of Churches would be a fair criterion of catholicity, were it not for the sad, though understandable, fact that the Roman Catholic Church has not yet been able to join that organization. It is interesting that the British Council of Churches dissolved itself in order to regroup in a form that allowed for Roman Catholic participation.

Genuinely world religions are few in number. Indeed, it has been claimed that Christianity is the only truly world religion. That is probably unfair to Buddhism and Islam, but hardly to the others. The indigenous religions of China and Japan are largely restricted to those far eastern countries and their expatriate peoples. The indigenous religions of Africa seem to be tribal in their very essence. Hinduism, despite its openness and internal pluralism, is too tied to Indian history and culture to be a genuinely world faith, except in highly esoteric philosophical forms which could never fuel the devotion of ordinary people. Jainism, too, is very much an Indian affair. The Sikhs, for all the purity of their ethical monotheism, are very much a particular people, stemming from the Punjab.

The Jews are, of course, a world-wide phenomenon; but their faith is so much tied to their being a particular chosen race that they make no universal claims on others and remain content to embody a special divine vocation in and to the world.

Buddhism, notwithstanding its Indian origins, has been one of the most successful missionary faiths, establishing itself in the Himalayas and Sri Lanka (as it now is), and throughout South-East Asia, China and Japan, and the appeal of its meditative techniques and its serene spirituality has become considerable in the western world as well. Any doubts about Buddhism will not be over its status as a *world* religion so much as about its status as a *religion*. For it lacks, indeed repudiates, such central features of religion, as most widely understood, as belief in the objective reality of God.

Islam is surely the strongest other candidate for the status of a world religion. Stemming from the same roots as Christianity, it claims to represent a further and final stage in the history of divine self-revelation. Its relatively simple ethical monotheism, with its capacity to evoke unshakeable faith and commitment and to order human life at both the individual and the social levels in a highly practical way, has not only shaped the destiny of the middle east, large areas of the Indian subcontinent, the former Soviet Union, Indonesia and Africa, but also made considerable inroads into black America and won a surprising number of converts in the west generally. Islam, too, has a long, impressive history of art and architecture and of scholarship. Admittedly, in its more fundamentalist forms it seems tied to the history and polemics of post-colonialism, uncritical of its own scripture and tradition, barbarous in its treatment of offenders and minorities, and oppressive of women. But these all-too-visible features of the contemporary Muslim world do not belong to the essence of Islam. In its purer, more enlightened, forms, Islam will prove an increasing challenge to western decadence and a powerful alternative to Christianity among the world religions.

Christianity, too, began in the middle east and its central doctrine of the incarnation – the claim that God himself, in the Person of the divine Son, lived out a human life in that place and at that time – bestows upon Christianity a 'scandal of particularity' greater than that of any other 'world' religion. But a decisive step was taken when the early Church broke away from its Jewish roots and threw its membership open to any and all who were attracted by its message of the boundless love, forgiveness and transformative power of the triune God. From its middle-eastern origins, Christianity could have spread in any direction. Indeed it was taken to south India in relatively early days. But the framework and communications of the Roman Empire inevitably meant that the main spread of Christianity would be westwards, and we have already mentioned the key role of Europe in the providential development of world-wide Christianity. The fact that the most significant growth points for Christianity today are Africa and Latin America can itself be read, in providential terms, as indicating the limited, temporary, role of Christian Europe on the way to a more extensive world-wide Christian catholicity.

The historical rivalry between Christianity and Islam for the allegiance of men and women in many parts of the world has been appallingly ugly and cruel – very much a part of the problem of evil at the heart of the religious world. In some places – certain multiracial cities in modern Britain, for example – the urgent need for practical co-operation on issues of race-relations and social justice has been discovered and acted upon by representatives of the various religious communities, including the Christian and the Muslim, with very positive results. This suggests the vision of a future where these different faiths are rivals only in the sense of offering for free acceptance or rejection, entirely in the spirit of tolerance and respect, different comprehensive views of the ultimate context and destiny of human life. The only criteria by which to judge these matters will be the ethical fruitfulness, social as well as personal, of these faiths and the plausibility of their respective claims to truth. And, of course, these two criteria are linked. In Christianity's case, the personal and social ethic that it offers to the world is inextricably bound up with its vision of the triune God and of the grace and love of God manifested in the incarnation. This is what is offered to the whole world by the Christian Church and this is what is exemplified – to some degree – by Christian individuals and Christian communities from every nation. It is in this world-wide presence and this universal offer that the catholicity of the Christian Church consists.

APOSTOLIC

The fourth characteristic or 'note' of the Christian Church is its unbroken line of continuity with Christ and his apostles. What this means in terms of the Church's ministry will be spelled out in the next section. But apostolicity is not primarily a matter of continuity in structure. Much more it is a matter of continuity with the faith and mission of the apostles. (The word 'apostle' means messenger, one sent out to proclaim the good news. Used first of the immediate disciples of Jesus, the twelve apostles, it also came to be used of other early leaders of the Church such as James, the brother of Jesus, who assumed the leadership of the earliest Jerusalem church, and, of course, of St Paul.)

Christianity, as has been stressed already, is a historical religion, not only in the sense that it has a long history but primarily in the sense that it transmits a historical revelation – God's self-disclosure through incarnation of his boundless love and forgiveness, evoking and creating a new mode of human being and human community in response. The first witnesses of that incarnation and its aftermath play an indipensable role in the coming-to-be of the Church; and the Church, if it is to be the Church, cannot lose contact with those founding events, or cut itself off from the faith of the apostles.

The matter is not as straightforward as it sounds, however. We do not have direct access to the apostles – or at least not to more than one or two of them, if that. Most of them, like Jesus himself, wrote nothing, and the earliest accounts of the events concerning Jesus Christ, including his teaching, were passed on by word of mouth. Only Paul's letters are unquestionably first-hand written evidence for the faith passed on to him from the immediate witnesses. It seems likely that the records of the beloved disciple, John, do lie behind the Fourth Gospel and the letters ascribed to him; but 'Matthew's' Gospel is probably a generation later, and letters ascribed to Peter later still.

The New Testament shows us the faith of the early Christians in varying stages of development, as the significance of Jesus' life and death and resurrection increasingly came home to those in whom the Spirit of Christ crucified and risen had come to dwell. As we have already seen, the Scriptures themselves contain only the raw material for a developed understanding of the Christian faith that first reached an agreed and fixed form in the creeds. These emerged over the first four centuries of the Christian era. But while they too play an essential role in transmitting the apostolic faith down the centuries, there was still much work to be done in drawing out their full implications and interpreting them in view of ever-changing and growing knowledge of the world. The development of Christian doctrine has been a never-ending process throughout the history of the Church.

But what God did in Christ does not change. The earliest written records of that divine act remain as Scripture, providing a fixed and permanent text for constant repetition and reflection in the worship and devotions of the Church and its members. And the early creeds of the undivided Church remain as the first considered summaries of the apostolic faith, recited every day in the liturgies of the Church and forming the starting-point for Christian theological reflection. Scripture and creeds are the given threads ensuring continuity across the centuries. Notwithstanding all the necessary developments and fresh interpretations, the Christian Church remains apostolic only if its life, mission and worship keep hold of those threads.

THE CHURCH'S MINISTRY

The apostolic faith is lived out, developed and passed on from
generation to generation by the Christian Church, the people
of God, the community of God's adopted sons and daughters.
We have already drawn attention to the key metaphor of the
'body' of Christ on Earth. That metaphor, as we have seen, was
spelled out by Paul in terms of different members fulfilling
different functions in the one 'body'. In an early development
of the metaphor, Christ himself is spoken of as the body's
head; and the question of leadership and authority in the
emerging Christian churches was bound to be an issue from
the very beginning. The fact that Jesus himself had selected
and appointed twelve disciples for a special role in the communication of his message was inevitably seen as a model for
the initial structuring of the Church, even when its leadership
was at first largely charismatic. Of course, the fact that Jesus'
own headship or lordship had been spelled out in terms of
ministry and friendship and had involved the way of suffering
love rather than the overt use of power was bound to affect
the kind of authority exercised by the early Christian leaders.
But there can be no doubting the leadership roles exercised
by James and Peter in the Jerusalem church and by Paul and
many others in the diverse Christian communities established
throughout the eastern Mediterranean world, and eventually
in Rome. In the New Testament period itself we see this taking
a more formal shape, with duly appointed offices of deacon
(minister), presbyter (elder) and bishop (overseer) emerging.

By the end of the second century, a more or less fixed
structure of Church order had evolved, with its threefold ministry of bishops, priests and deacons, with a certain primacy
being accorded to the Bishop of Rome. Certainly, something
of the informality of the early communities had been lost, but
that was inevitable as Christianity spread and developed into
what was to be a world religion. And, sadly, the style of Christian leadership became infected by more worldly paradigms.
This is an all-too-human story. But the example and the teaching of Jesus remained as an ever-present summons to a better
way.

A settled pattern of Church order, with new generations of

ministers commissioned by the Christian congregations or by their representatives and ordained by the existing leaders was a powerful symbol of continuity in the Church, just as the emerging papal primacy of Rome was a powerful symbol of the Church's unity. But it cannot plausibly be claimed that this structure is a necessary condition of the Church being the Church. For one thing, the Eastern patriarchs never accepted the sole primacy of Rome; and for another, the history of post-Reformation Christianity shows that the functions of ministry, representation, and oversight can be carried out in churches without bishops. Certainly the apostolic faith, which, as we saw, is the main criterion of continuity, has been passed on without the 'apostolic succession' of an unbroken chain of episcopally ordained ministers. All the same, it is hard to see, from a practical point of view, how any future united Church could fail to re-establish something like that threefold pattern, or at least recover a common episcopal order. Most ecumenists are also persuaded that such a united Church would almost inevitably endorse some form of constitutional primacy for the Bishop of Rome.

A word must be said at this point about the notion of priesthood as it applies to Christian ministry. This causes problems in a way in which the diaconate (the ministry of service) and episcopacy (the ministry of oversight) do not. Of course, in episcopal churches, bishops remain priests, and so the office and work of a priest is the basic form of specialist ministry in those churches. (Both bishops and priests, in a sense, remain deacons, but that is by the way.) I say specialist ministry, because there is a broad sense of ministry in which all Christians share in the Church's ministry to the world. Indeed, there is a broad sense of priesthood in which we can and must speak of the priesthood of all believers. This is one of the growth points in the contemporary Church's self-understanding. The involvement of the laity in ministry, including the fostering, training and commissioning of specific forms of lay ministry and the participation of laity in forms of synodical government, is a highly positive development after centuries of clerical domination. But, for all that, the Church still calls – and believes that God has called – particular individuals to take on special functions of service, representation and oversight in the Christian body; and priesthood in the narrower specialist sense, from early days, has been the principal order of such ministry.

But what does priesthood in this context mean? The Christian priest is not like the Old Testament priests who offered expiatory sacrifices on behalf of the people. We saw, in chapter six, how that whole system was already challenged by the Psalmist and the prophets and decisively transcended by God's own self-sacrificial act of forgiveness and love in the life and death of Jesus, God the Son incarnate. There is no place for priests in that old sense in the Christian scheme of things. But, while the notion of expiatory sacrifice is gone for ever, the notion of offering remains. God still offers himself to us, and we are called and enabled to offer our lives to God. This latter point is what justifies talk of the priesthood of all believers. But, in addition to this universal self-offering of Christians to their God, there is the more special sense of priesthood as representation, where specially called and ordained ministers are authorized to represent the people in bringing their self-offering to God, and also, although this is more controversial, to represent Christ in communicating his gift of himself to all believers. More will be said about this in the next chapter on the sacraments, when we consider the centrality of the Eucharist in the life of the Church. But there can be no doubt that, throughout Christian history, at least in the mainstream churches, this notion of two-way representation has remained the key to the notion of Christian priesthood and the chief justification for the maintenance of priestly ministry in the Church.

There is much debate as to whether these offices were restricted to men in the earliest Christian communities. Some evidence certainly suggests otherwise. But for most of Christian history, the priesthood has been a male prerogative. It is true that some Protestant churches had long abolished any restriction of the ministry to men, but this was in the context of a view of ministry that tended to repudiate the representative function of Christian priesthood just described. It is a highly significant decision, therefore, that has been taken recently by the majority of Anglican provinces, including the Church of England, to open the priesthood to women. For

Anglicanism has preserved the historical threefold ministry of bishops, priests and deacons, and has embraced, in its prayer books and in its teaching, a theology of priesthood along the lines advocated here. What has made the ordination of women to the priesthood possible is not only the post-Enlightenment emancipation of women – a sociological factor, albeit rationally based, that certainly favours this move (just as older, irrational, sociological factors made it virtually impossible) – but, much more importantly, a thoroughly Christian and theological recognition that in Christ there is neither male nor female (Galatians 3.28) and that, in so far as the priest does represent Christ, it is the full humanity, not the maleness of Christ, that constitutes the essence of what is being represented. That Christ's maleness was irrelevant to his salvific role was acknowledged in chapter five when we discussed the recently agreed alternative translation of line 16 of the Nicene Creed: '. . . and became a human being'. It is equally irrelevant to the ministry of those who represent him. The ordination of women to the priesthood is therefore a great step forward in the history of the Church, and it is to be hoped and expected that other Churches, including the Roman Catholic Church – although clearly not in this millennium, as a certain Cardinal remarked – will follow the example of the Anglicans.

THE CHURCH'S WORSHIP

The Christian Church has four main functions to perform: to transmit the apostolic faith to all who are willing to hear and receive it, to express and perform humanity's explicit worship of the triune God, to shape the life of Christians at both individual and community levels in conformity with Christ and the blessed Trinity, and to work for a better world through service of those in need and through the quest for social justice in God's world. The bulk of this book is concerned with the first of these functions, although the third and the fourth – the ethical implications of the Christian faith – are also very much before our minds. Here, in this section, we consider the second of the Church's functions: the Church's worship. This is a theme to which we shall return in the next chapter on the sacraments, but some reflection in more general terms on the nature and point of the Church's worship is called for at this stage.

The theme has already been touched on in the chapters on the Trinity and the Holy Spirit, where it was pointed out how, according to the Christian scheme of things, humanity's explicit response of praise and adoration of God is both energized by God from within and taken into God's own triune life. Here the emphasis must be on the *Church's* role, on the fact that Christian worship is not so much an individual response as a corporate act of the redeemed community. Of course, individual Christians do make their own responses of thanksgiving and penitence and petition in their own personal prayers; but it is the calling of the Church as a body – as the 'body' of Christ in the world – to bring to a public and visible focus the conscious and explicit response of creation to Creator.

This is done in a variety of ways, most notably in the Divine Office, the regular daily services, said or sung, in monasteries, convents, cathedrals and parish churches all over the world. In many such places, this regular offering of worship is done by professionals on behalf of the wider Christian community, who themselves assemble as a body at most once a week to celebrate God's gifts and enlist God's succour for the world. As I say, the eucharistic aspect of this offering will be dealt with in the next chapter; but, whether the Church's offering takes a eucharistic form or not, and whether the Divine Office is said or sung by professionals or by the whole local Christian community, it is still a representative function, praise and worship being offered on behalf of the whole creation. The same is true of the many kinds of less formal worship that take place in schools, people's homes, or out in the open air.

Where belief in God is taken seriously, the response of worship will seem the most natural thing in the world. For our nature, what God has created us to be, is to know God and enjoy him for ever. Clearly, there will be an element in this of awe and reverence for the infinite, almighty, source of our and the world's very being; 'for in him we live and move, in him we exist' (Acts 17.28). But where *Christian* belief in the triune God of love and in God's self-revelation in Jesus Christ is taken seriously, worship will be much more a celebration of that love, and a letting of that love reflect back from its image in us to its source in God. In a nutshell, Christian worship is the celebration of the love of God.

Precisely as such, the Church's worship is the point at which we draw on the resources of the divine Spirit for all the tasks of character building, community building and service of the world that constitute the third and fourth functions of the Church listed above. We cannot celebrate the love of God without letting that love inform our lives, as individuals and as a body. This was quite clear to St Benedict when he drew up his rule for the monks of the Benedictine order. The regular liturgical round equips the monk for the communal life of the brotherhood and for the service of the world. But the same pattern obtains in Church life more generally. Regular worship equips the Church to be the Church and to be God's primary instrument in the sanctification of the world.

THE CHURCH'S TASK

Worship, then, like the faith itself whose meaning I am exploring in this book, equips the Church for its task in the world. But what is that task? Well, much has already been said about this, as I have tried to bring out the ethical import of what is believed about God and the revelation of God's love, and as I have tried to expound the nature of the Holy Spirit's sanctifying work. But, in a chapter on the Church, I need to pay particular attention to the Church's own common life, to the kind of community or fellowship that the Spirit of Christ crucified and risen makes possible and real in each locality where groups of Christians meet together not only for prayer and worship and not only to serve and help to humanize the world around them, but also to realize and enjoy a special kind of common life. In a way, the Church's task is just to be the Church, to be a fellowship of Christian love, reflecting back something of the inner-trinitarian divine communion, and anticipating, to some degree, the eventual communion of saints, which is creation's destiny.

The famous exclamation, 'See how these Christians love

one another', might have been meant sarcastically, and, as already acknowledged, there is much in Church life, past and present, to justify the sarcasm. But an authentic Christian church should, and sometimes does, manifest a particularly impressive kind of fellowship and community life, including utterly personal care for the young and the old and for those particularly afflicted, but including, too, the common celebration not only of the love of God but also of the joy of life and its creative possibilities. It is also, in essence, a peaceable community, forbearing from litigation, and seeking at every point the way of forgiveness and reconciliation.

Some Christian ethicists go further than this and urge that authentic Christian communities should embrace the cause of pacifism, bearing witness to a better way than that of the resolution of disputes by resort to war. But, while the witness of Christian pacifism is something to be respected and honoured as a pointer to what is undoubtedly a key element in the fruit of the Spirit, namely peace, it is difficult to see how the Church can insist on its members always following the path of pacifism and of conscientious objection in time of war. For such are the responsibilities of Christians as citizens and indeed of the Church at times as the conscience of the nation – on this there will be more to say in the next section – that the only way to secure a just peace will be to participate in a just war. Just war theory is, of course, as much concerned to impose limits on the belligerence of nations and on the way in which war is waged as it is to defend innocent victims and throw back the aggressor.

This notorious ambiguity in the Church's commitment to the cause of peace makes clear once more the fact that authentic Christianity cannot shut itself off from politics and seek simply to create ideal forms of communal life wholly isolated from the secular world within which it is placed. Some further reflection, therefore, is called for both on the Church and the nation and on the Church and the world.

THE CHURCH AND THE NATION

For better or for worse, the human world is divided into a large number of nation states. This is inevitable, given the size of the Earth, its geographical subdivisions, and the long histories of ethnic continuity, migration, war, and the rise and fall of empires. Some nations have natural and obvious frontiers, others are quite arbitrary. Some consist largely of a single racial stock, though most have a thoroughly mixed ancestry and even those who do not are liable today to include substantial minority groups among their citizens. We saw in chapter one how potent a factor on the human scene is a sense of national identity, often contributing greatly to the vitality of a culture and to a people's sense of worth, but also often fostering inter-communal conflict that occasionally, as in the Balkans, reaches horrific proportions.

Religion has had its part to play in this, again for good and ill, and, among the religions, Christianity has had its share in fomenting and sustaining international strife and civil war. The so-called wars of religion, moreover, were between allegedly Christian nations, Roman Catholic and Protestant.

But what *should* the relation be between the Church and the nation? If Christianity is ultimately concerned with the sanctification of the world, it cannot ignore or bypass the fact that the world consists of nation states and that these form the immediate political context of every particular church body. The Church will certainly hope to reinforce the positive and humane side of national identity as well as to work for the greater permeation of society by Christian values. But it is bound to take up a critical stance towards all those aspects of the state that make for intolerance, injustice and strife. Here the Church is indeed the conscience of the nation. Where, instead, it supports and reinforces those evils, its betrayal of its calling knows no bounds. And, in any case, the Church, in essence, is an international, world-wide, body, with an overarching loyalty to one whose authority 'does not belong to this world' (John 18.36). For this very reason, the Church is bound to support such international organizations as the United Nations and its agencies, and while, given the fearful history of war in Europe in the twentieth century, it will be inclined to favour European integration, it will, in its more critical mode, oppose an inward-looking European policy that enriches the European community at the expense of the poorer nations.

In most parts of the world, including Europe, the various denominations of the Christian Church have no official status. They exist, increasingly, alongside other religious communities and secular groups as private bodies, possessing no more than moral influence within the states in which they find themselves. They have *had* to learn the lessons of tolerance and co-operation that ought to have been seen to follow from their own internal basic principles. But in some countries, for historical reasons, there remains an official link between the Church and the nation. There remains, in some form, a state or established church, be it Roman Catholic, Lutheran, Presbyterian or Anglican. The question arises whether this is a good thing or a bad thing, a relic of the conditions that, in earlier centuries, fostered the excesses of nationalism or even the wars of religion. Many Christians think it better to cut these ties completely. The Church can be the Church, internally and in relation to the nation, much more authentically and responsibly if it has no official status in, or ties with, the state. Surely its critical function and its world-wide horizon are better served by total disestablishment.

But there are a few things to be said in favour of some residual establishment where history and demography make this still appropriate. For an official tie does give a church a number of opportunities to serve the nation in ways not otherwise possible. The Church's concern for the institutions of government, education and welfare is signified if these retain something of an officially Christian nature, and, more importantly perhaps, the Church's concern for the whole of life is signified and made more effective where its ministrations at key moments in human life are made officially accessible to all. Increasingly these functions are being carried out, as they must be carried out, with proper sensitivity to other interested parties, whether religious, ecclesial or secular. But there is something to be said for a parish system which gives all people access to the Church's ministrations as of right.

A good example of the way in which an established church can minister to the nation's needs in a particularly sensitive area was the Thanksgiving Service in St Paul's Cathedral, London, for the British victory in the Falklands War. By the criteria usually applied this had been a just war; but the religious service of thanksgiving was tempered not only by prayers for those bereaved on the British side but also for those on the Argentinean side; and the then Archbishop's address was notable for its sensitivity and lack of triumphalism. Here the established church served the nation well.

THE CHURCH AND THE WORLD

The world, as I say, consists of nation states, but the Church's concern for the world is both narrower and broader than its concern for the nation. Narrower, in the sense of its concern for individuals in their need. Love of the neighbour has always been seen as the hallmark of any Christian fellowship which seeks to follow the example of its Lord. And those particularly in need have always elicited Christian practical compassion in evidently non-utilitarian ways. The mentally handicapped, the lepers and the blind, are cared for simply on the basis of their need. The hospice movement – for the care of the terminally ill – is of particular Christian inspiration.

But people's needs in large part reflect the social and political conditions in which they find themselves, and we have already seen how the Spirit's sanctification of the world involves the Church in concern for the wider structures of society. The imperative to help to make the world a better place cannot possibly be interpreted in terms of charitable work alone. The just order of society, both nationally and internationally, is of direct concern to the world-wide Church of Christ in all its particular branches. Clearly, at this level, we are speaking of moral influence and practical co-operation with individuals, communities and organizations of any faith or none. We have already noted the wide scope of the Spirit's hidden, mediated, activity, beyond the explicit Church itself.

Of course, there is a negative, pejorative, sense of 'world' in which the Church is always opposed to the world. So-called 'worldly' values – materialistic, egoistic, at best utilitarian – are indeed to be challenged by any authentically Christian ethical teaching. Here the Church resumes its critical role at each and every level – individual, social, national and international. This is the vertical dimension of God's law of love, which challenges humanity to question its own values and achievements on any worldly plane or scale. But there is another sense of 'world' in which the Church is committed to the world as God's world: to the world, that is, of family and society, of nations and communities of nations, of human culture and artistic creativity – all of these aspects of creation being part of the good work God is doing, and all of them having a place in the final consummation of God's creative plan, of which I shall speak in chapter ten.

And, since the world is not simply the human world, we must include at this point a reference to the other-than-human values of creation which it is also the Church's task to protect, to reverence and to celebrate. The beauties of the natural world, the inherent value of each animal species and of plants, trees, rivers and mountains, and the whole ecological interlocking system of nature, are to be cherished, not solely as instrumental to human well-being, but for their own sake as part of God's good creation. In all these matters the Church of Christ has an interest. It is entirely appropriate to find a Christian presence both in the patronage and encouragement of the arts and in movements for conservation.

THE CHURCH AND THE KINGDOM OF GOD

The kingdom of God is that future intended end-state of creation where God will unambiguously reign, and God's will will be done. Of course, 'kingdom' is a metaphor and we saw, in chapter five, how such notions of sovereignty get heavily qualified in the light of the revelation of God's searching love in Jesus Christ; and some people may well prefer the terminology of 'the communion of saints', which has already been used to characterize the perfect conformation of the human world to Christ and the blessed Trinity. But, sticking to the 'kingdom' terminology for the moment, we recall how, in the Lord's Prayer, we are taught to pray, 'thy kingdom come, thy will be done on Earth as it is in heaven'. But of course the final realization of God's kingdom will not be on

Earth. God's kingdom will only be fully present in heaven. So what does the Lord's Prayer really mean? It means that, in the power of the resurrection, something of that future kingdom can be realized on Earth. The Church's prayer is for the Spirit indeed to sanctify the world, and, in so far as Christian men and women and the Christian community are conformed to Christ, there exists here on Earth an anticipation and 'earnest' of God's kingdom.

We cannot equate the Church and the kingdom, but in so far as the Church is enabled to fulfil its true nature, it can be regarded as a foretaste of God's kingdom. In the Lord's Prayer we plead that more and more of God's world, as a result of the Church's witness and work, but also as a result of the Spirit's wider activity in creation, will be brought within the sphere of God's 'kingly' rule. The Church's task is to be the conscious spearhead of that process and the explicit sign of its real possibility. But the Church is always pointing ahead to the future full realization of the kingdom in heaven. When that 'day' comes, there will be no more need for the Church. It will become the communion of saints in God's perfected 'kingdom'.

CHAPTER NINE

Sacraments

WHY SACRAMENTS?

When the Nicene Creed, after affirming belief in one holy catholic and apostolic Church, continues, 'We acknowledge one baptism for the forgiveness of sins', we might wonder whether we are still concerned here with the *essence* of Christianity. Certainly, the forgiveness of sins is essential to the Christian faith, but why baptism? And why, if the Christian sacraments are to be mentioned in the Creed, is there no reference to the Eucharist, the central act of Christian worship, which surely belongs even more closely to the heart of Christianity?

No doubt the reference to baptism has something to do with the fact that, initially, the Nicene Creed was the profession of faith made at their baptism by those newly adopted into the 'body' of Christ. But I shall take the reference to baptism at this point in the Creed to symbolize the sacramental nature of the Christian religion and I shall expand the discussion to include some treatment of the Eucharist and other sacraments. Naturally, the main focus will be on the spiritual realities signified and conveyed by the sacraments, but the importance of the fact that in Christianity these spiritual realities *are* both signified and conveyed sacramentally is the principal theme of this chapter.

Christianity speaks of 'the great mystery of the incarnation', and initially the Latin word *sacramentum* was used to render the Greek *mysterion*. Just as in the incarnation itself, God's self-communication to humankind takes a visible embodied form, so in the sacraments God's grace is effectively embodied in outward and visible signs. There are two elements in the definition of a sacrament. Sacraments are not only 'outward and visible signs of an inward and spiritual grace' but are also, as the Anglican Articles of Religion put it, 'effectual signs of grace' in which God 'doth work invisibly in us, and doth not only quicken, but also strengthen and confirm our faith in him'.

There is a great appropriateness in the fact that an incarnational religion like Christianity should express itself and perpetuate itself down the generations in an incarnational manner. Earlier, in the chapter on creation, it was pointed out how the whole physical universe acts as a kind of screen between Creator and creature, allowing the latter to acquire its own identity by being set at a distance from God and rooted in a natural world, which gives it independence and a life of its own. But, as well as setting us apart from God, physicality becomes, through the incarnation, the very medium of divine communication, and that same principle lies behind the sacraments. Physical elements, instead of separating us from God, become the vehicle and means of our union with God. Water symbolizes and, under the prescribed conditions, becomes the effective means of the mystical washing away of sin. Bread and wine symbolize and, under the prescribed conditions, become the effective means of Christ's real presence in, and gift of himself to, his 'body', the Church.

BAPTISM

The use of water in a ritual of symbolic cleansing was already a feature of certain strands of Judaism at the time of Jesus. John the Baptist used it after summoning people to repentance and to prepare themselves for the coming of God's kingdom. It is remarkable that Jesus, who needed no repentance and who was himself the bringer of God's rule, submitted to John's baptism, presumably as a mark of solidarity with the sinful humanity he had come to serve and to save. But Christian baptism in the threefold name of the triune God differs from John's baptism in that this symbolic cleansing now becomes the effective sign of the Holy Spirit's embrace. This rite of

Christian initiation claims for each new member of Christ's 'body' not only the divine forgiveness shown and enacted by Christ himself but also the Spirit's sanctifying power. That taking into the divine life, of which we wrote in chapter seven, is both signified and initiated in this rite of Christian baptism.

The first Christians were, of course, adults responding consciously and gladly to the message of the Gospel; and it is understandable that many Christians today are minded to reserve this rite of explicit Christian initiation for the time when a person can make such a response self-consciously in the full knowledge of what he or she is doing. But, from early days, whole families were welcomed into the Church, and eventually infant baptism became the norm. This powerfully symbolized the fact that the initiative in our salvation rests with God, that we do not have to earn it, that the divine forgiveness antedates even our repentance. As we saw in chapter six, it is the costly love and forgiveness of God, incarnated in Jesus to the point of crucifixion, that in the end wins our response and elicits our repentance, opening our lives up to the interior working of the Holy Spirit. It came to seem quite natural and appropriate for the Church to claim all this in advance and by anticipation for new members of the human family. In any case, as we have seen, the Church is primarily a corporate affair, not just a set of individuals.

Of course, once infants were welcomed, by anticipation, into the family of the Church by baptism, provision had to be made for those baptised in blissful ignorance of what was being done to them and said on their behalf to make their own profession of faith at a later stage when able to embrace the Christian fellowship and the Christian gospel for themselves. The sacrament of confirmation will be discussed in a later section of this chapter, but clearly there is room for a variety of rites to mark some further stage of actual commitment or indeed repeated renewal of baptismal vows. But as we shall see, it is pointless and confusing to speak of a fresh baptism. The public rite whereby a particular person is set apart from evil and placed within the already operative sphere of God's forgiving love – even when performed solely in anticipation and hope – cannot be repeated.

Infant baptism comes to seem even more problematic in a

secular age, when families with little contact with the Church still seek baptism for their children, whether through pressure from older generations or through some residual 'folk-religious' sense of a need to celebrate a new birth, the first 'rite of passage'. Again, it is understandable that some churches attempt to discourage or even to ban this practice. But the pastoral consequences of a strict baptism policy are disastrous. People become even more alienated from the Church and from religion if they find themselves rebuffed in this way. It is far better to use requests for baptism as pastoral opportunities to welcome even the most tentative approaches and to reflect something of the boundless love of God even for those largely alienated from the Church. And if baptism does indeed both signify and convey something of the prior actuality of God's forgiveness and God's grace, it can still be used to embrace a new child of God and potential Christian even in relatively unpropitious circumstances. As urged throughout this book, the Spirit's work is not limited or restricted to the company of fully self-conscious and committed Christians. In any case, a sensitive and welcoming response to a largely ignorant request for baptism gives the Church the chance to do something towards removing that ignorance and mediating God's love.

FORGIVENESS

The Creed makes it clear that the spiritual grace sacramentally signified and conveyed through baptism is the forgiveness of sins. That God's forgiving love comes first and is freely given – at great cost to God in the crucifixion of God's incarnate Son – has been the fundamental guiding motif behind this exposition of the Nicene Creed. As was made clear in chapter six, God's forgiveness in no way has to be earned. Admittedly it has consequences: it wins our response; it makes clear that we have to learn to forgive; it opens the way to the Spirit of the living God to come into our hearts and into our midst to energize Christians and the Church into being the community of those who know that they are forgiven. But none of this is a prior condition of God's forgiveness and in any case none of it happens all at once. The act of baptism simply proclaims the divine love and claims it for another human person.

It follows that we cannot possibly suppose that the forgiveness of one's sins depends upon one's having been baptized. The fact that generations of Christians worried about the fate of unbaptized infants is a sad reflection of the way in which the Christian faith was taught. Of course, one way or another, God's human creatures have to learn that they are forgiven and accepted by the God who made them, and baptism is the divinely ordained way of proclaiming that fact and conveying its reality, even if only by anticipation. But no sacrament is a necessary condition of salvation. Sacraments are simply special, God-given, visible, ways in which the spiritual realities of an incarnational religion are passed on. It is not necessary, but it is supremely fitting, that through baptism, the divinely ordained rite of Christian initiation, the forgiveness of sins should be both celebrated and applied.

Sin is a deep and serious business. No human being can escape its bondage whether at the personal or at the social level. In one sense of the word 'natural', self-centredness is quite natural to humanity in the making. Of course, many people have a 'natural' benevolence and positive regard for other people too, but these virtues are precarious in a wicked world – not only vulnerable to the greed and anger of others, but at risk of internal distortion and corruption in the most good-natured of human beings. This results as much from social pressures which impose themselves on people, inclining them to participate, despite themselves, in rank injustice and disregard. Worse still, people get corrupted and enslaved by perverse ideologies and caught in structures of evil to an appalling degree. It is not difficult to see the point of the old idea of original sin, when we recognize the all-pervasiveness of these tendencies that constitute a large part of the social world into which every human child is born.

Forgiveness is an even deeper and more serious business. Into our alienated world came the incarnate Son to bring God's forgiving love, suffering in person the consequences and the burdens of our fallen state, taking upon himself the pains of rejected love to the point of crucifixion. In the ways described in chapters six and seven, this frees us from both guilt and bondage, enabling us to accept that we are accepted and adopted into God's family. In Paul's vivid metaphor, we die to sin and rise to righteousness, as the Spirit takes us into the Church's fellowship, enabling the power of the resurrection to begin to take effect in the human world.

Baptism is the public, overt, sacramental rite by which these spiritual realities are claimed for new human beings, often ahead of their actual conscious participation, but setting them explicitly within the family circle of the Church for all that.

ONE BAPTISM

The Creed, following Ephesians 4.5, asserts the Church's acknowledgement of *one* baptism for the forgiveness of sins. This reference to the unity of baptism can be understood in two ways. The first is the fact already mentioned that the Church is commissioned to perform this sacramental act once and once only in the case of each new member, irrespective of whether it is a case of infant baptism or believer's baptism. Only once is a human individual publicly initiated, sacramentally, into the Christian 'body', even if, as in the majority of cases, this is done in hope and anticipation. It is part of that hope, of course, that there will be many occasions in the future when the Holy Spirit will inspire and energize that person consciously to fresh acts of commitment and participation in the Church of Christ and its work in the world; but, while such moments may be signified through some other sacrament or rite, the Church does not re-baptize. The initial claim and proclamation, however anticipatory, is made – and recorded – once and for all.

The idea of a second 'baptism in the Spirit' is just confused. It is a misuse of the word 'baptism' as the Church has come to understand it in carrying out the Lord's command. The Fourth Gospel's contrast between John's baptism and Christ's baptism cannot be transferred to a supposed contrast between 'water' baptism and 'Spirit' baptism in the Christian Church. By the sacramental principle, Christians believe the Spirit to be present and active in baptism as such; and that means baptism with water in the threefold name. Moreover, it is not

just the Church here on Earth that claims the divine forgiveness and the gift of the Spirit for each new member in baptism.
We believe that explicit membership of the Christian family is
actually conferred by God the Holy Spirit in and through the
sacramental act of baptism – even though the personal appropriation of that gift may be still to come.

The second way in which the Creed's reference to 'one'
baptism may be understood depends on the once-for-all nature
of this act of Christian initiation being respected in every
denomination throughout the Christian world. It is a prime
mark of the Church's unity that, despite all differences and
divisions, this one sacramental rite of baptism by water in the
threefold name is accepted by all Christian churches as the
God-given way of explicit initiation into membership of the
'body' of Christ on Earth.

THE EUCHARIST

The Eucharist is the supreme Christian sacrament, so much
so that receiving the consecrated bread and wine can be
called 'receiving the sacrament'. Unlike baptism, which
happens only once and whose effect is only initiated in the
way outlined above, the Eucharist is celebrated repeatedly,
and through it Christians, as individuals and as a fellowship,
are spiritually nourished again and again by the very life and
presence of their Redeemer and sustained in their membership of Christ's 'body', the Church.

The Eucharist, we are told, is many things at once. It is a
memorial of Christ's passion and death. It is, as its name
derived from the Greek suggests, a thanksgiving for what
God in Christ has done for us and for our salvation. It is an
anticipation and a foretaste of the heavenly banquet – the
communal celebration of God's completed work in the end.
But, above all, it is the special mode of communion between
believers and their Lord, whereby the risen Christ makes himself present to his followers and takes up their feeble offering
of themselves and their world into his own perfect offering of
an all-inclusive human life to the Father. I say 'all-inclusive'
because it is indeed Christ's taking of *humanity* into God with
which we are associated, through baptism and communion,

in the fellowship of the Church. This is why the Eucharist is first and foremost a corporate affair, not just a personal 'communing' between an individual believer and the Lord. All the movements for liturgical reform and renewal, in the Roman Catholic Church, the Anglican Church, and the other Protestant Churches, have emphasized this corporate dimension. The central altar, the gathering round the Lord's table, the participation of the whole congregation in the rite, reinforce this emphasis on the Eucharist as a family celebration. Even sick communions – the taking of the sacrament to those unable, through illness or incapacity, to attend the common worship of the gathered community – are a means of associating the housebound or those in hospital with the fellowship of the local church who have met together to break the bread and meet their risen Lord precisely as his 'body' here on Earth. And even where the Eucharist is celebrated – early in the morning or in a distant, isolated, place – by a priest together with only one or two fellow Christians, this is still not a private, personal, act of devotion. It still represents the whole 'body', the 'many' who at other times and in other places are performing this same sacramental act that nourishes and sustains the Christian Church.

Let us consider now the two most difficult and controversial aspects of the Christian Eucharist, the eucharistic sacrifice and the real presence of Christ in the Eucharist – aspects over which the Church was sharply divided at the Reformation and about which the different denominations have been struggling to find a common mind ever since.

It will be clear from our reflections on the notion of sacrifice in chapter six that we cannot think of the Eucharist as in itself an expiatory or propitiatory sacrifice. Only in the thoroughly moral sense of sacrifice as self-sacrifice can the Eucharist be supposed to possess a sacrificial character. There are, as we saw, two sides to this: Christ's sacrifice of himself for us and our offering of our lives to God through him. Both are symbolized and re-enacted in the Christian Eucharist, where bread and wine, representing first our own feeble offering of our lives to God, become the effective sign of God's gift of himself to us in Christ. By eating and drinking what now signify Christ's very life, we are made one with him, and our lives are taken with him into God.

It must be evident that while the priest indeed acts as the representative of the people whose offerings of bread and wine are brought to the altar, it is only in a minimal sense that he or she represents Christ himself in repeating the words spoken by him at the Last Supper. For the central focus of the rite is not the priest but the consecrated bread and wine which now signify Christ's body and blood, the very life of Christ, and mediate it sacramentally to the people. This brings us to the second aspect of the Christian Eucharist that has caused so much difficulty and controversy in the Church; namely, the real presence of Christ in the Eucharist.

We can understand the difficulties felt by the Reformers over the medieval doctrine of transubstantiation; the idea that, as the words of consecration are spoken, the bread and wine suffer a hidden but substantial change into the body and the blood of Christ. But equally the sacramental character of this divinely instituted rite is surely lost if we suppose it to be nothing but a symbolic remembrance of things past or a prefiguring of the heavenly banquet to come. Rather, the mainstream Churches have come to see that what lies behind the medieval doctrine of transubstantiation is the valid recognition that, by divine ordinance, the consecrated bread and wine of the Eucharist mediate a special encounter with Christ crucified and risen that is nowhere else available. Christ is sacramentally present to and in the Christian community gathered round the altar as nowhere else this side of eternity. This is the God-given way by which Christians are enabled to participate in the very life of Christ. And if we are serious about the sacramental principle that spiritual realities are effectively conveyed by physically embodied signs, then we can see the point of reserving the sacrament, not only to be taken to the sick, but also for public and private devotion; always remembering, however, the primary context of eucharistic worship in which we, as the Christian fellowship, receive Christ's 'body' and 'blood' not only into our midst but into our very selves, as we are united with him and drawn into the life of Christ.

Many churches in our time have rediscovered the centrality of eucharistic worship. A number of reservations, however, have been expressed about this on the grounds that it tends to restrict the Church's worship to those with degrees of faith, commitment and understanding that some people, not only on the fringes of the Church, feel unable to acknowledge. Certainly it is important to encourage other forms of worship as well, ranging from choral evensong to more informal services, in which varying degrees of participation are possible. The same may be said of carol services and many other special corporate acts of thanksgiving or remembrance. But, of course, there will be varying degrees of understanding and commitment among participants in eucharistic worship, and, as with baptism, it is unwise to set conditions for communicant status too high. Traditionally, confirmation has been regarded as a precondition for admission to communion; but there is a strong movement in the Church to relax this and allow at least the children of church families to receive communion long before the age of fully self-conscious commitment and consent. The Roman Catholic policy of relatively early confirmation has much the same effect, although this could be seen as involving unrealistically early professions of explicit faith. In many ecumenically minded church bodies the Eucharist is thrown open to members of all the Churches without too much enquiry into what, beyond baptism, constitutes membership.

Such open policies do not necessarily suggest a lax or careless attitude to Christian faith. They reflect, rather, an awareness of the priority of grace and of the fact that a growing faith is more a product of participation in the life and worship of the Christian community than its precondition. If sacraments are indeed effective visible signs of the presence and activity of the Spirit and of Christ, then the Church will be unwise to try to impose too strict a condition on their accessibility.

Eucharistic worship, like baptism, belongs to the essence of Christianity, not in the sense that the spiritual realities signified – Christ's presence in the Church, and the Holy Spirit's embrace – are wholly dependent on these sacramental acts, but in the sense that Christianity simply would not be the incarnational religion that it is without these visible embodiments of spiritual grace at work. Moreover, baptism and the Eucharist are held to be the peculiarly God-given ways by which membership of the Church and spiritual sustenance in the Church are provided.

OTHER SACRAMENTS

Where the so-called five 'lesser' sacraments of confirmation, penance, orders, matrimony and (extreme) unction are concerned, only the last named shares the relatively unconditional efficacy that has just been claimed for baptism and the Eucharist. To anoint the sick or the dying with oil is one way of claiming and expressing in visible form the spiritual power of the living God, whether to bring healing or to sanctify the passage from this life to the next. In the nature of the case the spiritual resource thus signified operates in part at least below the level of consciousness. But the other four sacraments are, in their various ways, sacraments of commitment and cannot seriously be supposed to operate at levels other than that of fully self-conscious decision.

Confirmation through the laying on of hands (usually by the bishop) marks the stage where an individual Christian publicly affirms in person the commitments made on his or her behalf at baptism. Where infant baptism is the norm, some such ceremony clearly is required. It was suggested above that it is better to separate confirmation from the question of admission to communion, in which case it makes sense to delay confirmation until early adulthood. While the churches differ in their practice and understanding of confirmation, it is usually held that the solemn public laying on of hands constitutes another outward and visible sign of an inward and spiritual grace – a fresh gift of the Holy Spirit at a public moment of personal commitment to Christ and his Church.

The sacrament of penance – the performance of a specific, albeit token, act of contrition following confession of sin and the pronouncement of absolution by a priest – has been treated as a sacrament throughout much of church history, and one can see the point of some such outward sign of the reality of the divine forgiveness operative in a person's life. But such are the dangers of setting conditions on the divine forgiveness that the practice of penance has fallen into disuse in many branches of the Church and cannot plausibly be claimed to belong to the essence of Christianity.

Where the threefold ministry of bishop, priest and deacon is maintained, the conferral of these orders is also widely regarded as a sacrament. As with confirmation, the bishop lays his hands on the candidates, men and women whom the Church believes to have been called to the ministry and who have been duly trained for the task, and publicly invests them with the office and authority in question. Again, as with confirmation, the inward and spiritual grace of a fresh gift of the Spirit is believed to be imparted in and through this sacramental rite. Patterns of ministry vary, however; and, while the functions of ministry, as we saw in the last chapter, are indeed essential to the Christian Church, it is probably unwise to insist on a single form and a single rite. The sacramental principle applies, no doubt. The Spirit of God works in the Church through publicly commissioned ministers; but, as with all the 'lesser' sacraments, a greater variety of practice is both actual and acceptable within the world-wide Christian Church.

The Church is even more divided over whether marriage should be regarded as a sacrament. Unlike all other sacraments, the parties themselves here are the ministers, making public vows of life-long commitment, symbolized by the giving and receiving of a ring (or rings). Certainly, the Church has an interest in supporting and blessing marriage and the family as a divine ordinance for the well-being of human beings in society. But is the marriage rite itself a means of grace? One might hope so. But certainly it differs from rites which belong to the Church's own life and task as the worshipping, celebrating, witnessing and serving people of God in the world.

So there are bound to be some reservations about the old idea of seven sacraments, structuring the Christian life from the cradle to the grave. Depicted in the beautiful and moving sculptures of the seven-sacrament fonts that still adorn some of our country churches, that medieval view of the common sacramental life can hardly be claimed to belong to the essence of Christianity. Christianity is indeed both incarnational and sacramental in its very nature. The Church would indeed no longer be the Church if it abandoned the 'gospel' sacraments of baptism and the Eucharist. But, while many other rites and practices share the sacramental character of mediating divine grace through visible signs, their variety and lack of uniformity throughout the world-wide Christian 'body' militate against any further allocation of specific sacraments to the essence of Christianity or the Church.

A SACRAMENTAL UNIVERSE?

We have suggested that the sacraments are rightly seen as an extension of the principle of incarnation, whereby the divine grace is communicated to human beings in an embodied form. But this insight can be generalized to indicate a sacramental view of the universe as a whole. The physical universe, as well as acting as a screen between God's glory and the creatures made in God's image so that they are not overwhelmed by God and deprived of their autonomy as persons, at the same time mediates God's beauty and God's grace in many indirect and unexpected ways.

'The heavens tell out the glory of God' (Psalm 19.1): this classic text of natural theology reflects the widespread sense that the natural world, by its grandeur and beauty, bespeaks the reality and majesty of God. And, despite the terrible problem of evil which I attempted to face in chapter four, the natural world has, again and again, been held to reflect God's presence and power. Sometimes this takes a very vague and almost pantheistic form, as in the nature mysticism of Wordsworth, expressed in *Lines Composed above Tintern Abbey*. The poet felt

A presence that disturbs me with the joy
Of elevated thoughts; a sense sublime
Of something far more deeply interfused,
Whose dwelling is the light of setting suns,
And the round ocean and the living air,
And the blue sky, and in the mind of man;
A motion and a spirit, that impels

All thinking things, all objects of all thought,
And rolls through all things.

More succinctly and more powerfully, Gerard Manley Hopkins wrote, in *God's Grandeur*:

The world is charged with the grandeur of God.
It will flame out, like shining from shook foil;

The poem concludes:

And for all this, nature is never spent;
   There lives the dearest freshness deep down things;
And though the last lights off the black West went
   Oh, morning, at the brown brink eastward, springs –
Because the Holy Ghost over the bent
   World broods with warm breast and with ah! bright wings.

This is one way in which a sacramental universe speaks to us of God. Another is through art and architecture and music. A Michelangelo sculpture, a Gothic cathedral, a Mozart piano concerto, can become to us the voices of creation, articulations of the deep meaning and beauty of the world and its creative possibilities. These were themes that I touched on in chapters five and seven when considering God's creation and the Creator Spirit permeating all things and inspiring artistic creativity as a special mode of imaging the divine. Here I underline the fact that all this demonstrates the sacramental nature of the universe which we inhabit, its capacity to produce, and to evoke, outward and visible signs of inward and spiritual graces at innumerable points in nature and the history of humankind.

God's visible, embodied, presence and activity in and through the created world is not limited to the incarnation or the sacraments of the Church in the strict traditional senses. There is a more widespread presence of the divine Spirit, as we saw in chapter seven, when reflecting on the positive role of the whole history of religion and ethics in making something of God's reality and God's nature known to the human world. Here we acknowledge an even more general, universal, presence and activity of God in and through the sacramental universe itself.

This insight can be pressed too far, as it is by those who speak of the world as God's 'body'. This blurs the Creator/creature distinction and fails to do justice to the transcendence and the otherness of the triune God. On a sacramental view of the universe it is precisely the *created* world – that is, that which is other than God and wholly dependent on God for being in being – that becomes the vehicle and the medium of the triune God's immanent presence and activity. Equally, a Christian theology of nature will not be happy with the opposite view – to be found most powerfully expressed in Islam – that, such is the transcendence of God over the created world, that there can be no association between God and nature of the kind which Christians affirm in their sacramental view of the world and especially in their doctrine of the incarnation.

SACRAMENTS AND THE INCARNATION

I return, therefore, to the central Christian doctrine of the incarnation, which is, as it were, the lynchpin holding together and controlling what Christians say about the whole universe being sacramental on the one hand and what they say about the particular Church sacraments on the other.

The sacramental view of the universe that we find in the Hebrew Scriptures was already complemented by a powerful theology of God's Word. The psalm that affirms that the heavens tell out the glory of God affirms too that 'the precepts of the Lord are right and give joy to the heart'. And it was the prophetic books, with their insistent 'thus saith the Lord' that shaped and refined the faith of Israel into the eventual context for the incarnation much more than the theology of nature and of art reflected in Genesis and the Psalms. In the fullness of time it was the divine Word who became flesh and dwelt among us (John 1.14). This supreme sacramental mystery of God's embodiment in a human life was effected by the Holy Spirit, that same Spirit who, in Hopkins' words, broods over the bent world; but it was the Word, the divine Son, who was and is the subject of the life and acts and teaching of the incarnate one. The Son of God's embodied presence in the world as Jesus was therefore a far more explicitly personal and articulate presence than the intimations of divinity in things that captivate the minds of poets, ancient and modern. All the same, the incarnation focuses and brings to a providential culmination a sacramental principle that was there from the beginning, was recognized by the wisdom writers of ancient Israel, and is still perceptible to poets and mystics today.

The sacraments of the Church continue this same principle in focused form. Moreover, the Holy Spirit's embrace in baptism and the real presence of Christ in the Eucharist are guaranteed by divine promise in a way in which the intimations of divinity in nature and art are not. The latter are unpredictable and gratuitous, albeit indicative to those with eyes to see of the fact that God is everywhere; but anyone baptized with water in the threefold name is in a position to know for sure that he or she is an accepted member of Christ's 'body', God's people here on Earth; and anyone who comes to the Eucharist with even a modicum of faith is in a position to know for sure that the risen Christ is there to be received in holy communion. This kind of assurance can be extended to sacraments like confirmation, penance and orders; for the Church of God has the authority and commission to proclaim through some outward act the priority of grace and the reality of fresh gifts of the Spirit, where people offer themselves to God from commitment, penitence or a special sense of vocation. And where unction is used, its efficacy as a sign of God's healing presence to the sick or of God's loving embrace of the dying is equally assured. The same may doubtless be said of marriage where it does indeed possess the character of a real sacrament of commitment in the sight of God. God will surely bless such a union.

One note of warning should be sounded over such an understanding of the Church's sacraments, however. Conviction of their efficacy as signs and media of special gifts of God's own presence and power to Christians and the Church should not be converted into belief in some indelible character imprinted for ever on the recipient. At times, in the history of the Church, this has been held regarding orders, making it quite impossible for a priest to renounce his or her orders or to go through the full procedure of laicization. It has also been held regarding marriage, leading to conceptions of indissolubility that have had appalling pastoral consequences when marriages have in fact broken down and the question of a second marriage arises. These ideas depersonalize a sacramental religion and in any case lack clear meaning. The gifts of the Spirit, like Christ's real presence in the Eucharist, are thoroughly personal and not to be treated as a kind of magic. Even the once-for-all nature of baptism should not be thought of in this way. It is simply the Church's decision, in the light of the Lord's command, to signify the claim and embrace of the Holy Spirit in making someone a member of the Church by baptism once for all time. If they leave the Church and later come back, they are not re-baptized, for their basic membership has already been signified and recorded. They are welcomed back some other way.

ETHICAL IMPLICATIONS

The ethical implications of a sacramental view of the universe are much the same as those already sketched in chapter five regarding an incarnational religion. There, it was a matter of recognizing the ethical demands of the total involvement and the self-sacrificial love exemplified in the incarnation and the way of the cross. Here, the wider sacramental perspective suggests the same ethic of involvement; but in discerning the presence of the divine in the cosmos and the Earth, the sacramental view suggests not only an ecological sensitivity to the whole planet but also an expectation that God is to be found already at work in nature and in art as well as in the whole moral and religious life of humankind. Christians will, of course, insist that the sacramental view is controlled and shaped by the religion of the incarnation. They will not endorse any naturalistic ethic that goes against the love of God revealed in Christ. But the world to which the Gospel is preached and to which the Church bears witness by its life and by its love is not foreign territory to the God of the whole Earth.

Some thinkers have claimed to discern the principle of self-sacrifice manifested and enacted in the life of Christ, in nature itself, in the undeniable fact that life itself evolves and is passed on through the sacrifice of individuals and generations and even species. But this is a dangerous idea. It confuses the moral and personal ideal of self-sacrificial love with what in fact is part of the problem of evil. A theology of nature can be pressed too far. Something was said in chapter four about the necessities involved in the fashioning of a world of life from below. It is in the values that emerge from that structure that God's presence and God's will are to be discerned, not in such necessities of the structure as suffering and death themselves. Of course God does take these things upon himself in the cross of Christ, but only to draw their sting and overcome them. They do not themselves provide analogies for the divine love.

We have to hold on to the tension between the idea of nature as a barrier between God and ourselves, out of which we have to be drawn in order to enter the world of the spirit, and the idea of nature as itself the bearer and the vehicle of spiritual values. Spirit is not attained by leaving nature behind. It is realized rather through the transfiguration of nature, so that what was a barrier becomes the medium of grace. The ethical consequence of this sacramental view is that God's will is done not by flight from the world into a detached world of the spirit but by finding and working for the realization of spiritual values in and through a transfigured world.

THE CESSATION OF SACRAMENTS

Sacraments are a form of indirect communication. As we have seen, inward and spiritual grace is conferred through outward and visible signs. Just as the incarnation was the most appropriate way for the infinite triune God to reveal God's nature and will to humankind, so the sacraments of the Church are appropriate, embodied, means of divine presence and inward working in God's finite creatures in the making. Moreover, the physical world itself, as well as giving us our independence and identity as creatures, can become the means of divine disclosure and action. But while the Church has taught the permanence of the incarnation in that in Christ humanity is taken into God for ever, it has generally been held that sacraments will cease with the transition from here to eternity.

The reason for this is that the outward and visible world as we know it is a temporary feature of God's whole creative process. Only in its formative phase does creation possess this inevitable ambiguity, the conditions of our formation at once hiding God from us and at the same time able to become the vehicle of revelation and providence. As we saw in chapter five, the resurrection of Christ does not end this process of indirect communication. For history goes on and the risen Christ has to withdraw from the Earth until the end time. He is present to his Church only spiritually and sacramentally, the sacraments continuing the incarnational principle while we are still in the first phase of the story of creation. But, as we shall see in the final chapter when we consider the ultimate destiny of creation, resurrection takes us into the conditions of the new creation, where there is no more ambiguity. The nature which both conceals God from us and mediates God to us will have fulfilled its function, and creatures will find themselves directly face to face with their God. At that point the assimilation of incarnation and sacrament comes to an end; for the risen, glorified humanity of Christ will present God to us in an unconcealed and unambiguous way. This is the sense in which sacraments are temporary while the incarnation is permanent. Similarly, whatever we mean by the resurrection body and the resurrection world, they will surely lack the ambiguity that conceals God from us under present conditions. So the need for sacraments will cease.

CHAPTER TEN

The Last Things

THE RESURRECTION OF THE DEAD

The last two clauses of the Nicene Creed express the Christian hope and expectation of a perfected consummation to God's whole creative plan in the end. This dimension to the Christian faith certainly belongs to its essence. Without it the event which launched the Christian movement, the resurrection of Jesus Christ, would be unintelligible; and the problem of evil and suffering would be quite insoluble. Whatever explanation may be hazarded for the presence of evil and suffering in God's world would certainly not justify creation at such a cost (even if that cost were inevitable), unless creatures, fashioned so arduously from below, had an eternal destiny in store for them. But, in any case, if there is anything that can reasonably be claimed to constitute a divine promise in the teaching of Jesus, it is that the dead will be raised.

As I try to tease out what might be meant by the resurrection of the dead, I note first that this belief or hope is inextricably bound up with belief in God and indeed in the objective reality of God. Christian conviction that there will be a life beyond death is not based on philosophical speculation or on anthropological study of what it is to be a human being. Christians are not committed to belief in the immortality of the soul quite apart from belief in God. From a merely natural or human point of view, it seems quite clear that humans, remarkable though their mental, rational and spiritual capacities are as products of nature, are inherently mortal, just as other animals are. The higher capacities, including human subjectivity, that distinguish us from other animals, are so bound up with the complex neurophysiology of the brain that brain death has quite properly become a criterion of the death of the person as a psychological whole.

I shall return to the subject of death in a later section of this chapter. The present point is simply that Christian belief in life after death is derived from beliefs about God, not from beliefs about humans. God's power, God's nature and God's promises are the basis for the ultimate Christian hope: God's power, because only the infinite, omnipotent, Creator has the power to recreate finite beings made in God's image; God's nature, because it is the boundless love of the triune God, revealed in the incarnation and the gift of the Spirit, that ensures that God will not let his personal creatures go for ever; and God's promises, because conviction that God will raise the dead is not just derived from reflection on God's self-revelation in Jesus, but actually declared in the teaching of Jesus himself.

Not that belief in the resurrection of the dead was a new idea stemming from the teaching of Jesus and from experience of *his* resurrection. The faith of Israel in its post-exilic developments had already come to embrace this conviction, largely as a result of reflection on God's justice and God's faithfulness in times of disaster and persecution. The belief was contested in Judaism at the time of Jesus, as we see from his disputes with the Sadducees; but for most Jews the expectation of resurrection had come to form the ultimate horizon of their hope. And it was that expectation that made it possible for the disciples to experience the first Easter as Jesus' resurrection and a foretaste of what was to come for all.

In trying to say what is meant by the resurrection of the dead, we are bound to follow closely what was said in chapter five about the resurrection of Jesus. Resurrection cannot be thought of as the reanimation or reconstitution of the physical body that has been buried, cremated or committed to the ocean. It is a new creation, a restoration of the deceased person in a new mode of being. We shall receive an incorruptible, glorified 'body', just as the resurrection 'world' will be a new, unambiguous and imperishable environment. But the question immediately arises, if it is not the same physical stuff which constituted our earthly body that is raised in a transformed and exalted condition, what is it that continues from this life to the next, so that it is indeed we, and not just a set of replicas, who inhabit the new creation?

We are at once driven back to the idea of something like the soul – not as an inherently immortal substance, but as the spiritual centre of our personal existence and subject of our activity and interpersonal relations, which transcends its physical base and becomes capable of receiving the gift of resurrection. It is, perhaps, the greatest of the mysteries of nature that evolution has produced a highly complex animal organism that not only comes to possess mental states and spiritual capacities but also becomes a *subject* of thought and action and interpersonal relation. Christian belief in resurrection involves the supposition that such subjects can be and will be re-established in being after death through 'embodiment' in a new resurrection 'body', and a new resurrection 'world', where the community of those raised to be with Christ will find an everlasting home.

THE LIFE OF THE WORLD TO COME

In a later section of this chapter, we shall have to ponder the temporal nature of this expectation of a life beyond or after death. It certainly looks like hope for an ultimate *future* state, if the last clause of the Creed is anything to go by. And, indeed, much has been made already in this book of creation as a process yet to be completed, and of history as a linear development pointing to a future goal. Reflection on creation and the problem of evil led to the suggestion that finite persons could only be fashioned gradually from below, in and through an evolving world that provides us with the conditions of relatively independent existence and growth. Only such a creative process can be genuinely self-reproducing and thus creative of new persons. And, of course, for new generations to come into being, former generations must pass away and die. It follows that if people from every generation, including all life's victims, are to participate in the intended goal of creation, the culmination to the whole story cannot possibly be supposed to take place within history. It can only occur beyond history through a new creation in which all participate by resurrection.

More will be said, in a later section on heaven, about the nature of this future consummation. Here I single out just some of the basic, constitutive, features of what the Creed calls the *life* of the world to come.

The life of the world to come is the intended destiny of all those finite persons fashioned gradually and indirectly in and through the Earth and its multifarious history. Once fashioned in this way, persons and communities of persons become susceptible of eventual transference into the conditions of eternity; conditions which will lack the ambiguities and frustrations of the present formative phase. But it is quite clear that the Creed envisages a new *life* beyond the grave. It is not a question of *this* life being viewed by or retained in the memory of the triune God. God raises the dead to new life, and, since there can be no life without continuing experience and activity, that must mean new unending experience of bliss and fellowship and new activity through exploration, discovery and creativity, and through fresh works of love.

Much has been made throughout this exposition of the Creed of the way in which humanity is taken into God through the incarnation of the divine Son or Word and through the inspiration and indwelling of the Holy Spirit. The horizon and context of the life of the world to come will therefore be the trinitarian life of God, focused unambiguously in the risen Christ, who is the human face of God for ever. This lack of ambiguity is an important aspect of the life of the world to come. I have already mentioned it in connection with the cessation of the sacraments in the final consummation. There will be no more need for indirect communication. But is also needs to be stressed that the unambiguousness of the future life accounts for the fact that there will be no further risk of creation falling away from the divine intention.

If the triune life of God constitutes the ultimate horizon and environment of the life of the world to come, this does not mean that finite spirits, raised to life eternal, will lack a *created* environment or world. On the contrary, I have repeatedly referred to a resurrection *world*, the imperishable created environment in which the life of the blessed is lived. This is what is meant by 'heaven'. But of course it is not given to us in this life to know in any detail what heaven will be like: 'Scripture speaks of "things beyond our seeing, things beyond our hearing, things beyond our imagination, all prepared by God for those who love him"' (1 Corinthians 2.9). All we can do – and I shall attempt this shortly in the section on heaven – is develop certain intimations of eternity that are given to us in moments of rapture such as those of ecstatic love, aesthetic creativity or wonder, or mystical experience.

There are a number of reasons why we should resist the suggestion that Christian hope for a life beyond death is a matter of wish fulfilment. For one thing, many people, including some Christians, do not wish for it. For many, a limited lifespan is quite enough. And most people can think of plenty of individuals whom they would not wish to be confronted with in a world to come. If there is a reputable wish behind the Christian hope of heaven it has nothing to do with selfish interest. It is a wish for justice and redress for the vast multitudes of life's victims. In any case, as already pointed out, the hope of heaven is based not on anything of ours, but rather on the divine promises.

The accusation that unending life would be boring can be given equally short shrift. It reflects an astonishing poverty of the imagination. On no account can the life of the world to come be thought of as an endless extension of this life as we know it here on Earth. To share in the infinite creativity and love of the triune God, without any of the frustrations attending the circumstances of our formation on Earth, is bound to transcend utterly the conditions in which it is possible to be bored and is bound to be endlessly fulfilling and absorbing.

DEATH

I turn now to consider the traditional 'four last things' – death, judgement, heaven and hell. I have already acknowledged our mortality in the context of this first formative phase of God's creative plan. We are indeed among the higher organisms with a limited lifespan of, on average – at least in the west – of some seventy years. Death is perfectly natural; it is impossible, in an evolutionary perspective, to think of it as a consequence of the fall or as a punishment for sin. Many lives are cut short in their prime, however; and this raises the problem of evil once again; although the value of brief lives is undisputed. Jesus himself was put to death at about thirty-three years of age, and, as Ben Jonson puts it, 'In small proportions we just beauties see; And in short measures, life may perfect be'. The deaths of small children are much more harrowing and, as already pointed out, it is the fact of countless entirely, or almost entirely, frustrated human lives that raises the problem of evil as much as anything and suggests the moral necessity of resurrection, if this world is indeed the creation of a God of love.

But we should not think of death just as a regrettable necessity in the context of the formation of new persons in and through an evolving world of biological organisms with inevitably limited lifespans. The bounded nature of life on Earth contributes to the specific values that make human life the poignant and fascinating thing it is. There is a strange ambiguity here. The values of childhood, of learning and discovery, of first love, of work and recreation, of family life, and of artistic creativity, but also the values of culture and civilization more generally, are all bound up with beginnings and endings, with the temporary, circumscribed, nature of all experience and activity here on Earth. And yet those very values, including all flowerings of goodness, beauty and truth point beyond themselves to an absolute ground which, when revealed as love, becomes the basis for belief in resurrection.

It is only the secular mentality – and the secular anthropology founded upon it – that insists on absolutizing the boundedness of human life, and refuses to consider the possibility that death is not the end. For Christian theological anthropology, by contrast, the formative phase of a human life, from conception to death, is seen as but the first phase in a creative plan that then involves resurrection, new creation and an eternal destiny. Indeed, we must affirm that it belongs to the essence of Christianity to hold that death is not the end. Death, judgement, heaven and hell are the four *last* things only in the sense that they come at the end of the first phase of God's plan. Subject to what will have to be said about judgement and hell, death is rightly seen in the Christian scheme of things as but the gateway to the life of heaven.

From time to time one encounters the assertion that the phrase 'life after death' is self-contradictory. This usually turns out to involve sheer stipulation – that death simply means the end of everything for the one who dies. Christianity rejects that stipulation as wholly unjustified. In the light of belief in God and in God's self-revelation, we learn, rather, that death is a moment of transition – the end of one phase and the beginning of another in the overarching purposes of God. But sometimes the idea of 'life after death' is rejected, not by definition but in the context of a conviction that the time of the space–time universe in which our lives on Earth occur is all the time there is. Since there is clearly no life after death as far as the ongoing history of the world is concerned – Christianity has nothing to do with spiritualist superstitions or belief in ghosts – we cannot, on this view, meaningfully speak of anything 'after' the story of our lives on Earth is concluded. This more serious threat to the intelligibility of talk of life after death will be dealt with in a separate section, below, on the whole theme of time and eternity.

JUDGEMENT

The notion of a last judgement, depicted so fearsomely in medieval and renaissance art, sums up the seriousness with which the Christian tradition has taken human moral responsibility. The idea that we shall all be held to account for our thoughts and deeds and characters, and that there will be no possibility of concealment or excuse when we are brought face to face with the penetrating gaze and the absolute justice of our Maker is a powerful religious idea – a mark of human dignity as well as an incentive to confront the truth about ourselves. But, as we saw when considering the role of Christ as judge, we cannot rest content with a picture of judgement which drives a wedge between the justice and the love of God, or which postpones judgement to a final, single, 'day' or reckoning at the end of history.

The Fourth Gospel speaks of the way in which people are judged already by their reaction to the coming of the Son of God into the world (John 3.18). The thought behind this saying is that love incarnate either wins our love in return or shows up our alienation and aggression. Moreover, without any specific act of punishment, that latter reaction tends towards ruin. The point can be generalized; for the love revealed in Jesus is in fact the law of the whole universe. It is written into the nature of things that rejection of God's law of love brings retribution on itself. Both people and nations tend to spiral into self-destruction if they persist in flouting that law.

Even prior to special revelation this fact can be perceived. It can precipitate moments of self-knowledge, leading to repentance in dust and ashes. The revelation of divine love reinforces all this. Some people cannot take that revelation, so they crucify it. But others are convicted of the truth about themselves, and let the divine love reshape their lives and their communities, and through them – hopefully – the human world.

It follows that judgement is best seen as a process, an ever-present and recurring, negative or positive, possibility. And it is very difficult indeed, if the divine love is really at the heart of things, to suppose that this process comes to an end at death. Of all traditional Christian beliefs, the decisiveness of death, in the sense that the human will is fixed irrevocably for good or evil at death, has surely become one of the least morally and religiously plausible aspects of the tradition. Many Christians may well feel that to abandon it goes against the thrust of both Scripture and tradition. But the case for giving up the view that there are no further opportunities for conversion and repentance after death is strong. This matter is certainly controversial. It will be pursued further in the sections on hell and purgatory below. For the moment, I simply register the fact that the morally persuasive force of the revelation of the divine love appears to be unending, this side of death and beyond.

What, then, is left of the idea of the Last Judgement and of judgement as one of the four last things? The picture remains, I think, a powerful symbol of the fact that, sooner or later, human individuals and human communities have to face up to the truth about themselves and reckon with how far short they fall of the divine intention. Only so can the resources of the divine love become available for the reconstruction of human life and human community, both here and in the world to come. Moreover, there is, after all, an element of finality in the picture. It may not realistically be locatable either in history or at death, but eventually a time will come, with the perfected consummation of God's creative plan, when truth will prevail and the divine love will have succeeded in reconstructing God's creatures, for all eternity, in the image and likeness of the triune God. In its final and ultimate sense, the last judgement will be the judgement that love has prevailed, that all is well, and that God is all in all.

HEAVEN

This leads us to further reflections about that ultimate consummation of all things known in the Judaeo-Christian tradition as heaven. Not that the word 'heaven' is reserved for the final state of God's perfected new creation in the end. We have already had cause to refer to heaven as the realm of the blessed dead and the 'place' where the risen Christ is now located at the right hand of God. The new creation is already in being, even though it is as yet incomplete. The ancient view that souls wait in the sleep of death until the Last Day when all are raised at once is incompatible with Jesus' words to the penitent thief on the cross, 'today you will be with me in Paradise' (Luke 23.43), as well as with everything that the Church has wanted to say about the risen Christ himself. So it makes most sense to think of the two great phases of God's creative plan – the formative phase of life on Earth and the recreative phase of the life of heaven – as overlapping. Finite persons, fashioned in and through the conditions of worldly, historical, existence, are taken into the new conditions of eternal life, perhaps gradually – we shall consider this in the section on purgatory below – and in any case during the preliminary stages of the creation of heaven, which will only be completed at the final consummation when 'the old order has passed away' (Revelation 21.4).

Our present interest, in a section on the four last things, is with that final consummated state when the formative phase is over, the number of finite persons fashioned on the Earth complete, and any intermediate purgatorial process fully undergone. Within the limits of our unavoidable ignorance regarding this ultimate state, can anything be said to fill out, if only a little, those intimations of eternity mentioned in the section above on the life of the world to come?

First, we should recall the theological constraints within which the Christian doctrine of heaven is developed. Our destiny is to be raised with Christ and taken into the trinitarian life of God. The life of heaven is essentially a corporate affair – the communion of saints – and that must mean the communion of the redeemed with one another and with the triune God. The so-called beatific vision, or the vision of God, cannot therefore be interpreted in an isolated, individualistic way, extrapolated perhaps from the intense experience of the solitary mystic – although mystical experience may provide one clue to the nature of heaven. But the models and metaphors that we find in the Christian scriptures are much more social and celebratory, heaven being compared to a feast or a party or a homecoming. These images, too, require some qualification in the light of the fact that Christian celebration takes place, pre-eminently, in the context of worship. Despite what was said in chapter nine about the cessation of sacraments in the unambiguous conditions of the perfected consummation, it is eucharistic worship, at its best, that surely provides another leading clue to what the life of heaven will be like.

The Christian tradition, however, has gone on to develop other, equally corporate, metaphors from shared aesthetic experience, say in the performance of a great choral or orchestral work. But this communal emphasis should not be pressed to the exclusion of individual rapture, experienced in moments of artistic creativity or sheer aesthetic enjoyment of a picture or a poem. Like mystical experience, aesthetic ecstasy may afford a clue to the beatific vision.

But if God is love, human experience of love given, love received and love shared still more, must constitute the heart of what mirrors the divine and the chief clue to what it means to know God and enjoy him for ever in the life of heaven. It is a striking fact that imagery from sexual love has supplied much of the language used in devotional and mystical litera- ture from the Song of Songs in the Old Testament to the classic writings of the great Christian mystics. But of course the exclusiveness of sexual love has to be transcended and left behind if such language is to convey something of the spiritual reciprocity and interpenetration through which the triune love of God is both reflected and shared in the com- munion of saints.

Finite minds may well be troubled by the thought of the sheer number of created persons whose intended destiny is the life of heaven. It may well be felt to make no sense to speak of communion and solidarity in the heavenly sphere with billions. Here another scriptural metaphor may come to our rescue: the 'many dwelling-places' in his Father's house of which the Lord assured his disciples in the course of the farewell discourses in the Fourth Gospel (John 14.2). The values of human life which may be expected to be re-estab- lished in the resurrection world will presumably include a great variety of particular cultural, communal and interpersonal forms of life – from those of family life to those of civiliza- tion. And there is room for much speculation about which values in this formative phase of creation are in fact resur- rectable and which are inherently temporary and thus bound to be left behind, except in memory. It could be the case that some apparently temporary values – those of animal life, for example – will in some form have a share in eternal life through association with the lives and loves of human beings.

Finally, we need to stress that the consummation of all things in the life of heaven to which the Church of Christ looks forward cannot possibly be thought of, in static terms, as a fixed and frozen state of God's whole creative process, with no further experience, activity or life. As already urged, the life of the world to come, even – indeed especially – in its perfected state, must be an endlessly dynamic and variegated sphere of celebration, exploration, creativity, life and love. What this means in respect of time and eternity will be considered below.

HELL

But what about hell and the terrible prospect of everlasting
damnation for the incurably impenitent that used to form so
central a feature of Christian eschatology? For very good reasons this has come to be regarded as morally and religiously
incredible, at least if taken literally. There is no denying the
seriousness of free will and responsibility. As stressed throughout this book these are essential features of what it is to be a
person and part of a moral community. And there is no denying the terrible states of alienation and brutality that people
can inflict upon themselves and on each other, creating a
large part of the problem of evil. The loss and destruction
brought about by human wickedness, at both the individual
and the social level, are self-inflicted in the sense that they are
the inevitable consequence of human sin. But the question
before us now is whether such states of loss and alienation
can become wholly irredeemable and if so, whether they
persist for all eternity.

The problem is not resolved by the recognition that such
loss is not so much a punishment inflicted by offended justice as the consequence brought upon people by their own
perversity and obduracy. The idea of everlasting loss in a permanently irredeemable condition remains just as morally and
religiously implausible as the idea of everlasting punishment.
From any moral perspective, it would seem quite pointless –
indeed morally repulsive – to maintain in being such irre-
deemably lost creatures, and all the more so from a Christian
perspective – a perspective, that is, determined by the self-
sacrificial love of God revealed in Jesus Christ. So it is not
surprising that belief in *everlasting* alienation has faded away.
Any conception of the eternal consummation of all things
containing for ever such a dark, inexplicable, surd is simply
incoherent.

There are only two morally and religiously tenable notions
regarding the fate of persistent impenitence. One is the view
known – not too happily – as 'conditional immortality'. In
this view, human freedom and responsibility are such that it
is indeed impossible for God to prevent the incurably wicked

from self-destructing. People can render themselves permanently unredeemable, in which case they can only be allowed to go out of being. The picture language of hell and damnation, on this view, refers to the irreversible loss of the possibility of participating in the perfected end-state of creation. But the consequence of ultimate impenitence is not a permanent state of alienation. It is, rather, annihilation.

The other morally and religiously tenable view is known as 'universalism' – the view that in the end all God's personal creatures will be saved. This view, which had its representatives in earlier periods of church history, has steadily gained ground since the nineteenth century, at least as a matter of hope. Indeed it is a striking fact that the leading twentieth-century Christian theologians, both Protestant and Roman Catholic (namely, Karl Barth and Karl Rahner) both, guardedly, expressed this hope. On this view, the revealed love and patience of the triune God is such as to be bound, sooner or later, to win the response of everyone, even the most obdurate. Clearly, this does not occur during the lifetime of many here on Earth, so universalism certainly entails abandonment of belief in the decisiveness of death. There must be further opportunities – for conversion – beyond the grave. But we have already seen reason to question the decisiveness of death as an essential element in Christian belief.

It is not easy to choose between these two views – the view that hell symbolizes self-inflicted annihilation, and the view that hell is a state of alienation destined eventually to be overcome. When we focus our attention of the human world and the monstrous wickedness of those responsible for genocide and other unspeakably inhuman acts, moral realism suggests the implausibility of the hope that love and forgiveness will one day win them over and reconcile them to themselves and to their victims as well as to their God. But when we focus our attention of the boundless love of God enacted and revealed in the cross and passion of Christ, where God in the Person of his incarnate Son takes upon himself the consequences of human wickedness, it is equally hard to believe that that love will ever finally be defeated even in a single case. From such a perspective we appreciate the force of the old saying that 'Christ remains on the cross as long as the last sinner remains in hell'. Consequently, we may surely hold on to the hope that in the end all will be saved.

PURGATORY

From the previous four sections it will have emerged that, of the traditional four last things, only one, namely *heaven*, is the genuinely last or final state, and even heaven must be thought to embrace endless new beginnings. *Death* may come at the end of the first phase of our formation, but according to the Christians it is certainly not *the* end. *Judgement* is continuous until the final consummation, when all, we hope, will have come to themselves, accepted the truth about themselves, and allowed themselves to be reconstructed so that *hell* will be no more.

But something must be said about the intermediate state between death and the final consummation. That there must be some intermediate state is clear. Quite apart from what has just been said about the need for further opportunities for the impenitent to come to themselves, few will be ready at death for instantaneous translation to the 'place' where the risen, glorified, Christ and the saints enjoy unimpeded communion in the very heart of God. Even when it was widely held that death marked the final break with any fresh possibility of radical change, the larger part of the Christian Church believed that those whose wills were set in the right direction at the time of their death still required a period of purgation, like gold being refined in the fire, before they were ready to meet their Lord. This is the doctrine of purgatory, memorably portrayed in Newman's – and Elgar's – *Dream of Gerontius*. The doctrine of purgatory suffered eclipse at the Reformation because of its gross abuse in medieval Christianity where people were misled into thinking that money could buy off time in purgatory, but as in other spheres, the Reformers, in doing away with this abuse, allowed the baby to go out with the bath water. Belief in purgatory itself was no abuse, but rather a moral and religious necessity, as it has remained.

Once we allow ourselves to entertain the hope of universal salvation and thus to abandon the old idea of the decisiveness of death, a greatly enlarged conception of purgatory becomes inevitable. For now it is not just a question of the refinement of those whose wills had already begun to be conformed to Christ, but, much more extensively, a question of the gradual winning over of the obdurate. We may add the point that further opportunities will doubtless be required for people nurtured in cultures and civilizations beyond the reach of Christianity to grow into the triune life of God and come to recognize the central role of Christ for all divine/human relations.

All this means that resurrection to the life of the world to come is, for most human beings, a gradual process, only completed when, through God's patient providence and grace, they are ready to enter into the final state of heaven and enjoy the beatific vision as participants in the communion of saints. And that communion will itself be incomplete until the stories not only of the Earth but also of the intermediate state have come to a definitive conclusion.

TIME AND ETERNITY

Some attention must now be given to the vexed question of the relation between time and eternity. This whole discussion of the last things has been undertaken in the language of time. The Creed itself speaks of expectation: we look for the life of the world to come. Although at times we have glossed this as life *beyond* death, we have not hesitated to speak of life *after* death. And the linear view of God's creative process that we have used and defended throughout this book has entailed belief in a *future* consummation. Talk of an intermediate state refers of course to a temporal interval between death and the end time; and the end time itself, involving the completed and perfected life of heaven, has been deemed itself to include a temporal dimension, with endless possibilities of growth in knowledge, beatitude and love.

But many Christian thinkers have found it hard to take this temporal language literally. If our ultimate destiny is to be taken into God's eternity and if God's eternity is beyond time, then creatures too must find themselves translated into a non-temporal mode of being if they are truly to be taken into the life of God. It is not easy – indeed it may not be possible – to make sense of this view. If only this life has a temporal structure and if resurrection is to a non-temporal eternity, it is difficult to see how resurrected creatures themselves can be the subjects of anything, still less the subjects of new lives and loves in God. In fact, most advocates of this non-temporal view of resurrection take it to mean the holding and cherishing of this finite, bounded, human life, viewed as a whole, in God's eternal, all-embracing, 'memory'. But such a view does not begin to do justice to the *life* of the world to come, nor does it begin to meet the problem of evil, given the fact that the vast majority of human lives on Earth are frustrated and unfulfilled to a greater or lesser extent.

A more plausible attempt to retain the notion of God's non-temporal eternity embracing all created times, past, present and future, in a single comprehensive creative act is to differentiate between the eternal life to which creatures are raised and God's own infinite non-temporal eternity. On this view, creation will always be temporally structured, with an endless future beyond death – beyond the death of individuals and beyond the heat-death of the universe – involving a genuinely future consummation along the lines outlined above; a consummation, that is, still temporally structured, but precisely *that* endless future being embraced, along with all created times, in God's eternal 'present'. This certainly allows the life of heaven to be thought of as a real enrichment and fulfilment of finite creaturely life, with ever-new experience, both individual and corporate, of the eternal love of God. But it is still not easy to make sense of the idea of God, from outside time, creatively embracing all creaturely times, including now this endless, open, future of the perfected life of heaven.

This means that we are driven to set a question mark against the idea of *God's* eternity as essentially non-temporal. It has always been difficult to see how a non-temporal God can relate in an appropriate way to a genuinely open-futured creation. And, increasingly, it has been recognized that if God *knows* the future from the non-temporal standpoint of eternity, that future cannot really be open and undetermined. It was for these reasons that in chapter two, when considering the attributes of God, I hazarded the speculation that omniscience could not include knowledge of the future, if the future is genuinely open. Moreover, I suggested that to be able to create a genuinely open-futured world and to relate it in an appropriately temporal manner is something far greater than to posit in being a whole spatio-temporal world whose consummation is itself embraced in the one creative act. It was in this connection that I spoke of God's own 'primordial' time and of the trinitarian 'history' of God into which God's creatures are *gradually* being taken as a result of the incarnation of God's Son, the sanctifying activity of the Holy Spirit, and the resurrection of those made in God's image to everlasting life.

As already pointed out, this does not mean that we are treating God's time as part of the spatio-temporal structure of our world. Not even our own eternal destiny is to be thought of as simply continuous with that structure, since this spatio-temporal universe may well be destined for annihilation in the long run. All the same, the new creation must be thought of as coming *after* the old, the resurrection life with its own structures coming *after* our earthly lives. Again, it must be stressed that it is only in the context of our present physical universe that time is bound up with the kind of loss and decay that tempts us to think of God as outside time. But even the perfected life of heaven – the ultimate future of creation – will lack those features. Quite obviously, they have no place in the infinite, sempiternal, life of God.

Only if we allow ourselves to suppose there to be some analogy between our time and God's eternal time can we speak intelligibly of God's life and of God's love. The same is true of God's acts of creation, incarnation, resurrection and indwelling. And the dynamic conception of the endlessly fulfilling consummation of all things in heaven that I tried to sketch in an earlier section of this chapter reinforces the view that in the end we shall be taken into God's eternal time.

THE PAROUSIA AND THE CONSUMMATION OF ALL THINGS

In drawing these reflections on the 'last things' to a conclusion, I must recall what was said in chapter five about the Parousia, the final 'coming' or 'presence' of Christ in glory in the end time, when God's creative and recreative purposes will have been brought to their fore-ordained completion. If it is indeed Christ who both brings God into humanity and takes humanity into God, then our ultimate future in God will be focused or centred unambiguously in the risen Christ; for he is the human face of God and it is through him that humans in the end will see God face to face.

At the end of Dante's sublime poem, *The Divine Comedy*, dating from the first half of the fourteenth century, the poet is taken to the very height or centre of Paradise and there he beholds the whole universe like a single book held together in God:

> In that abyss I saw how love held bound
> Into one volume all the leaves whose flight
> Is scattered through the universe around . . .

As the poet gazes in wonder at the supreme light of God, God's triune being is revealed as three differently coloured but concentric spheres:

> That light supreme, within its fathomless
> Clear substance, showed to me three spheres, which bare
> Three hues distinct, and occupied one space:

> The first mirrored the next, as though it were
> Rainbow from rainbow, and the third seemed flame
> Breathed equally from each of the first pair . . .

But this rather abstract image of the triune God does not remain like that. The second sphere is seen to have a human form:

> The sphering thus begot perceptible
> In Thee like mirrored light, now to my view
> When I had looked on it a little while –
> Seemed in itself, and in its own self-hue
> Limned with our image . . .

As the poet struggles with this mystery of the human face of God, the vision ceases, but he finds his will and his desire in perfect harmony with the divine love:

High phantasy lost power and here broke off;
Yet, as a wheel moves smoothly, free from jars,
My will and my desire were turned by love,
The love that moves the sun and the other stars.

FUTURE HOPE AND PRESENT TASK

The Christian hope of a perfected consummation to God's creative plan in the endlessly rewarding life of heaven has seemed to some people only a distraction from the present task of making the world a better place. And many have feared that, if universalism is true and all will be saved in the end, we will cease to feel the urgency of the demands of love here and now. This latter fear can be laid to rest at once. Christianity is totally misunderstood if its ethical imperatives are held to stem from the desire to avoid damnation. Indeed, anyone who draws from the universalistic hope the conclusion that nothing really matters has not begun to understand the nature of the love that inspires the hope that in the end all will be saved.

The Christian hope, in so far as it really is Christian, far from distracting us from present tasks, inspires and energizes just such commitment to making the world a better place. This is because the Christian hope of heaven is entirely derived from the love of God revealed in Jesus Christ. Just as faith without love is nothing (1 Corinthians 13.3) and faith without works is dead (James 2.17), so hope without the works of love is strictly incoherent – and for the same reason. Both faith and hope are grounded in love. This is why St Paul deems love to be the greatest of the theological virtues, faith, hope and love (1 Corinthians 13.13). And he has already told us explicitly that there is no limit to love's hope (v. 7).

While Christian hope is grounded in the love of God, it inspires and energizes love in us. People who believe that life is ultimately meaningless may still commit themselves to making the world a better place, but they lack the motivation and the inner strength that come from faith and hope in the Word made flesh and in the indwelling spirit of God. Conviction that the world is a meaningful place, that God is actively at work in the Church and in the world, and that all human lives have an eternal destiny, is what enables Christians to love their neighbour as themselves. And such conviction makes a difference to the way in which the love commandment is obeyed. Christians do not ride roughshod over individuals in attempting to restructure the human world, but they persevere, with patience and confidence, in working for a more just world precisely because they believe that in the end all will be well. And their commitment to those who, by any merely human standard, are beyond hope is a mark of their discernment of a child of God in every human form. That discernment, and the commitment that goes with it, are a product of the love that springs from hope for a share in heaven for all God's children. So, far from distracting us from present tasks, our future hope makes clear what needs to be done, and keeps us in touch with precisely those spiritual resources that enable us to work the works of love.

Epilogue

In this book, I have tried to expound and explain the doctrines of the Creed in such a way as to show their plausibility and power as a summary of the truth – the truth about the origin of the world, the truth about the meaning of life, the truth about the spiritual resources available to humankind for the overcoming of evil and egoism, and the truth about the ultimate destiny of us all. It will be evident that, on this understanding, Christianity is far more than just a way of life, an inspiring ideal of how we might develop as persons, treat each other in our common life together, and construct forms of social, national and international life that meet human needs and enable people, communities and cultures to flourish. Christianity is all these things, but only because all these things follow from the truths about God, creation and the future, summed up in the Creed, and because they are made possible by the spiritual energies and resources to which the Creed points. Christianity is a practical religion, but the practice is a consequence of the theory. Above all, the practice is the result of the creative and recreative power of the God in whom Christians believe.

I have tried to present all this in a critical, reflective, way, taking account of our modern historical, scientific and philosophical knowledge. I have shown no sympathy for uncritical, superstitious or magical views of the Christian religion. This is not because of an uncritical, credulous, acceptance on my part of contemporary secular liberal attitudes. On the contrary, I have been equally critical of our modern world and of contemporary fashions. I have argued that we need to recover an all-embracing vision of the triune God who made the world and us, who came into our midst by incarnation as one of us to win us back to God, and who draws us into God's own triune life by recreating us and our common life, through the power of the Spirit, from within. But we cannot ignore science and history and the methods of critical enquiry. Christian faith is robust enough not only to withstand such criticism, but to grow and flourish under its scrutiny. It is all the more compelling if it is found capable of taking the measure of modernity, purging and re-thinking its own understanding of the world and human life in the light of modern knowledge, yet making better sense of things than modernity, in its secular forms, has shown itself capable of doing.

Part of my task was to answer widespread criticisms of Christianity. I noted six such criticisms, based on 1) contemporary secularism, 2) the alleged conflict between science and religion, 3) the facts of evil and suffering, 4) our critical historical consciousness, 5) the problem of other religions, and 6) the actual track record of Christianity. I have tried to respond to all these criticisms as I have worked my way through the successive clauses of the Nicene Creed.

Contemporary secularism is, in fact, not too difficult to challenge. Its inadequacies are increasingly evident as we contemplate the havoc wreaked by our over-confidence in merely human powers, by the pervasive moral relativism of our times, and by our consumerist, materialistic, culture. Moreover, contemporary secularism's complete lack of explanatory power leaves the existence of our world and our own place in it quite unintelligible. A robust, yet critical, Christian faith that affirms a God-given meaning and destiny for the world and for human life, and that anchors the value of personhood, community and culture in the creative and recreative power of God's love, is well placed to offer a much more inspiring and intelligible vision of the world and of the spiritual resources available to humankind than anything our secular friends can suggest.

The alleged conflict between science and religion is much exaggerated. A Christian doctrine of creation can easily accommodate, indeed it can learn from, the discoveries of cosmology and biological evolution. The biggest threat from science to a religious view of life comes from so-called 'cognitive science', the theory that lies behind the quest for artificial intelligence, modelling the human mind on an advanced computer supposedly able to simulate all human thought and action. Here, philosophical analysis can help to show the flaws in such a self-defeating scientific programme. The idea that a computer could ever feel, let along think, betrays a fundamental confusion about the very nature of consciousness, let alone mind and spirit.

The problem of evil is the greatest threat to Christianity. It is not easy to understand why God permits so much wickedness, pain and loss in the world as we know it. In the chapter on creation, I tried to show that God has good reason to fashion us indirectly from below, in and through a regularly-structured natural world that can cause us much harm as well as produce us and furnish us with all the values of embodied, finite, human life. And human freedom, necessarily rooted in such a world, is bound to be open to abuse and perversion. I argued that the goods of creation, and especially the good of free, finite, personal and interpersonal existence, are simply unobtainable any other way. The risks of the formative process are inevitable, even for omnipotence. But it is only the formative phase that is so tragically at risk. All suffering and evil will, in the end, be overcome. Life's victims will be recompensed in heaven.

Our modern critical consciousness has inexorably driven us to view the Bible, Church history, and Christian doctrine much more critically as products of human history under divine providence, rather than as the result of direct, unmediated, intervention. Even the incarnation – God's coming into human history in the Person of his Son as one of us – does not necessarily involve a direct bypassing of human history and human life stories. Resurrection and our future destiny in heaven are quite a different matter, of course. Here, we do have to speak of new creation and a taking of the creature into new, transformed, conditions, quite beyond nature and history. But I hope I have shown that our thought about these matters too can still be critical and rational.

The question of other religions is high on our agenda in

the modern world of global communication and global interaction. I have tried to show how a Christian theology of revelation and salvation can embrace the whole human story without either depreciating the faith and spirituality of men and women of other religious traditions or playing down the central Christian doctrines of the Trinity and incarnation. In the currently popular terminology, the understanding presented here is neither exclusivist (restricting salvation to Christians) nor pluralist (treating all religions as equally revelatory and salvific paths to blessedness) but inclusivist (embracing everyone, eventually, in Christ). But I hope my all-inclusive understanding of the action of the triune God in Jesus Christ and his Church can be seen to do justice to what this same God has done and is doing elsewhere in the world, and not only in the religious world.

The sixth criticism was a much more down-to-earth objection. Confronted by the many horrors perpetrated by the Church and by Christian groups and individuals throughout nearly two millennia, it is indeed difficult at times to sustain a vision of Christianity as the supreme witness to truth and love that it in essence is and in practice ought always to be. And yet the self-giving love of God, enacted and made known in the story of Jesus Christ, is the most basic of all realities and will, in the end, without overriding our freedom, come to embrace us all and shape our final destiny in God. And there are some signs of the presence and the power of that love in natural human goodness the world over, in deep spirituality and grace throughout the history of religions, and especially in faithful and loving Christian lives and Christian communities which do reflect explicitly something of that love.

It is not enough, of course, simply to answer criticism. A positive and constructive exposition of the Nicene Creed has to learn from the criticism, relate plausibly to modern knowledge, and achieve an overall consistency, not only with the facts that science and critical history have disclosed, but also, internally, between the various elements within the Creed. Moreover, such an exposition must be both morally credible and morally compelling. I do not mean that secular morality must have the last word. On the contrary, as I pointed out in chapter one, secular morality is in a state of some confusion.

It is the task of Christian ethics and Christian doctrine to sort out that confusion and show not only a better way, but a more convincing rationale behind that better way. But the resulting world view must be seen to be morally convincing and morally inspiring.

All these tasks I have attempted, admittedly within brief compass, to carry out in this book. I hope it will have become obvious that a book about the Nicene Creed is not just a book about an ancient text from over sixteen hundred years ago. Rather, it is a book about the love of God which underlies the very being of the world and of our lives, and holds out to us the promise of renewal for eternity. It follows that conviction of the truth of credal doctrine cannot possibly be a matter of theory alone. Certainly, I have stressed the theory that shapes authentic Christianity, but the proof is in the practice. And the truths I have been concerned to spell out here will only come home to readers when they encounter, in person, something of the boundless self-giving love of God in the people and communities with which they have to do, and, especially, in faithful Christian men and women, and in the fellowship and worship of the Christian Church.